T0091664

Scaling Python with Dask
From Data Science to Machine Learning

Holden Karau and Mika Kimmins

Beijing · Boston · Farnham · Sebastopol · Tokyo

Scaling Python with Dask

by Holden Karau and Mika Kimmins

Copyright © 2023 Holden Karau and Mika Kimmins. All rights reserved.

Published by O'Reilly Media, Inc., 1005 Gravenstein Highway North, Sebastopol, CA 95472.

O'Reilly books may be purchased for educational, business, or sales promotional use. Online editions are also available for most titles (*https://oreilly.com*). For more information, contact our corporate/institutional sales department: 800-998-9938 or *corporate@oreilly.com*.

Acquisitions Editor: Nicole Butterfield	**Indexer:** nSight, Inc.
Development Editor: Virginia Wilson	**Interior Designer:** David Futato
Production Editor: Gregory Hyman	**Cover Designer:** Karen Montgomery
Copyeditor: JM Olejarz	**Illustrator:** Kate Dullea
Proofreader: Arthur Johnson	

July 2023:   First Edition

Revision History for the First Edition

2023-07-19:   First Release

See *https://oreilly.com/catalog/errata.csp?isbn=9781098119874* for release details.

978-1-098-11987-4

[LSI]

Table of Contents

Preface

We wrote this book for data scientists and data engineers familiar with Python and pandas who are looking to handle larger-scale problems than their current tooling allows. Current PySpark users will find that some of this material overlaps with their existing knowledge of PySpark, but we hope they still find it helpful, and not just for getting away from the Java Virtual Machine (JVM).

If you are not familiar with Python, some excellent O'Reilly titles include *Learning Python* and *Python for Data Analysis*. If you and your team are more frequent users of JVM languages (such as Java or Scala), while we are a bit biased, we'd encourage you to check out Apache Spark along with *Learning Spark* (O'Reilly) and *High Performance Spark* (O'Reilly).

This book is primarily focused on data science and related tasks because, in our opinion, that is where Dask excels the most. If you have a more general problem that Dask does not seem to be quite the right fit for, we would (with a bit of bias again) encourage you to check out *Scaling Python with Ray* (O'Reilly), which has less of a data science focus.

A Note on Responsibility

As the saying goes, with great power comes great responsibility. Dask and tools like it enable you to process more data and build more complex models. It's essential not to get carried away with collecting data simply for the sake of it, and to stop to ask yourself if including a new field in your model might have some unintended real-world implications. You don't have to search very hard to find stories of well-meaning engineers and data scientists accidentally building models or tools that had devastating impacts, such as increased auditing of minorities, gender-based discrimination, or subtler things like biases in word embeddings (*https://oreil.ly/tqjth*) (a way to represent the meanings of words as vectors). Please use your newfound powers with such potential consequences in mind, for one never wants to end up in a textbook for the wrong reasons.

Conventions Used in This Book

The following typographical conventions are used in this book:

Italic
: Indicates new terms, URLs, email addresses, filenames, and file extensions.

`Constant width`
: Used for program listings, as well as within paragraphs to refer to program elements such as variable or function names, databases, data types, environment variables, statements, and keywords.

This element signifies a tip or suggestion.

This element signifies a general note.

This element indicates a warning or caution.

Online Figures

Print readers can find larger, color versions of some figures at *https://oreil.ly/SPWD-figures*. Links to each figure also appear in their captions.

License

Once published in print and excluding O'Reilly's distinctive design elements (i.e., cover art, design format, "look and feel") or O'Reilly's trademarks, service marks, and trade names, this book is available under a Creative Commons Attribution-NonCommercial-NoDerivatives 4.0 International Public License. We'd like to thank O'Reilly for allowing us to make this book available under a Creative Commons license and hope that you will choose to support this book (and us) by purchasing several copies (it makes an excellent gift for whichever holiday season is coming up next).

Using Code Examples

The Scaling Python Machine Learning GitHub repo (*https://oreil.ly/scaling-python-dask-code*) contains the majority of the examples in this book. They are mainly under the *dask* directory, with more esoteric parts (such as the cross-platform CUDA container) found in separate top-level directories.

If you have a technical question or a problem using the code examples, please email *support@oreilly.com*.

This book is here to help you get your job done. In general, if example code is offered with this book, you may use it in your programs and documentation. You do not need to contact us for permission unless you're reproducing a significant portion of the code. For example, writing a program that uses several chunks of code from this book does not require permission. Selling or distributing examples from O'Reilly books does require permission. Answering a question by citing this book and quoting example code does not require permission. Incorporating a significant amount of example code from this book into your product's documentation does require permission.

We appreciate, but generally do not require, attribution. An attribution usually includes the title, author, publisher, and ISBN. For example: "*Scaling Python with Dask* by Holden Karau and Mika Kimmins (O'Reilly). Copyright 2023 Holden Karau and Mika Kimmins, 978-1-098-11987-4."

If you feel your use of code examples falls outside fair use or the permission given above, feel free to contact us at *permissions@oreilly.com*.

O'Reilly Online Learning

O'REILLY® For more than 40 years, *O'Reilly Media* has provided technology and business training, knowledge, and insight to help companies succeed.

Our unique network of experts and innovators share their knowledge and expertise through books, articles, and our online learning platform. O'Reilly's online learning platform gives you on-demand access to live training courses, in-depth learning paths, interactive coding environments, and a vast collection of text and video from O'Reilly and 200+ other publishers. For more information, visit *https://oreilly.com*.

How to Contact Us

Please address comments and questions concerning this book to the publisher:

O'Reilly Media, Inc.
1005 Gravenstein Highway North
Sebastopol, CA 95472
800-889-8969 (in the United States or Canada)
707-829-7019 (international or local)
707-829-0104 (fax)
support@oreilly.com
https://www.oreilly.com/about/contact.html

We have a web page for this book, where we list errata, examples, and any additional information. You can access this page at *https://oreil.ly/scaling-python-dask*.

For news and information about our books and courses, visit *https://oreilly.com*.

Find us on LinkedIn: *https://linkedin.com/company/oreilly-media*

Follow us on Twitter: *https://twitter.com/oreillymedia*

Watch us on YouTube: *https://youtube.com/oreillymedia*

Acknowledgments

This is a book written by two trans immigrants living in America at a time when the walls can feel like they're closing in. We choose to dedicate this book to those fighting for a more just world in whichever way, however small—thank you. To all those we lost or didn't get to meet, we miss you. To those we have yet to meet, we are excited to meet you.

This book would not exist if not for the communities it is built on. From the Dask community to the PyData community, thank you. Thank you to all the early readers and reviewers for your contributions and guidance. These reviewers include Ruben Berenguel, Adam Breindel, Tom Drabas, Joseph Gnanaprakasam, John Iannone, Kevin Kho, Jess Males, and many more. A special thanks to Ann Spencer for reviewing the early proposals of what eventually became this and *Scaling Python with Ray*. Any remaining mistakes are entirely our fault, sometimes going against reviewers' advice.[1]

---

1 We are sometimes stubborn to a fault.

Holden would also like to thank her wife and partners for putting up with her long in-the-bathtub writing sessions. A special thank you to Timbit for guarding the house and generally giving Holden a reason to get out of bed (albeit often a bit too early for her taste).

Mika would additionally like to thank Holden for her mentorship and help, and give a shout-out to her colleagues at the Harvard data science department for providing her with unlimited free coffee.

## CHAPTER 1

What Is Dask?

Dask is a framework for parallelized computing with Python that scales from multiple cores on one machine to data centers with thousands of machines. It has both low-level task APIs and higher-level data-focused APIs. The low-level task APIs power Dask's integration with a wide variety of Python libraries. Having public APIs has allowed an ecosystem of tools to grow around Dask for various use cases.

Continuum Analytics, now known as Anaconda Inc, started the open source, DARPA-funded Blaze project (*https://oreil.ly/FyqwQ*), which has evolved into Dask. Continuum has participated in developing many essential libraries and even conferences in the Python data analytics space. Dask remains an open source project, with much of its development now being supported by Coiled (*https://oreil.ly/BMLuP*).

Dask is unique in the distributed computing ecosystem, because it integrates popular data science, parallel, and scientific computing libraries. Dask's integration of different libraries allows developers to reuse much of their existing knowledge at scale. They can also frequently reuse some of their code with minimal changes.

Why Do You Need Dask?

Dask simplifies scaling analytics, ML, and other code written in Python,[1] allowing you to handle larger and more complex data and problems. Dask aims to fill the space where your existing tools, like pandas DataFrames, or your scikit-learn machine learning pipelines start to become too slow (or do not succeed). While the term "big data" is perhaps less in vogue now than a few years ago, the data size of the problems has not gotten smaller, and the complexity of the computation and models has not

---

1 Not *all* Python code, however; for example, Dask would be a bad choice for scaling a web server (very stateful from the web socket needs).

gotten simpler. Dask allows you to primarily use the existing interfaces that you are used to (such as pandas and multi-processing) while going beyond the scale of a single core or even a single machine.

 On the other hand, if all your data fits in memory on a laptop, and you can finish your analysis before you've had a chance to brew a cup of your favorite warm beverage, you probably don't need Dask yet.

Where Does Dask Fit in the Ecosystem?

Dask provides scalability to multiple, traditionally distinct tools. It is most often used to scale Python data libraries like pandas and NumPy. Dask extends existing tools for scaling, such as multi-processing, allowing them to exceed their current limits of single machines to multi-core and multi-machine. The following provides a quick look at the ecosystem evolution:

Early "big data" query
 Apache Hadoop and Apache Hive

Later "big data" query
 Apache Flink and Apache Spark

DataFrame-focused distributed tools
 Koalas, Ray, and Dask

From an abstraction point of view, Dask sits above the machines and cluster management tools, allowing you to focus on Python code instead of the intricacies of machine-to-machine communication:

Scalable data and ML tools
 Hadoop, Hive, Flink, Spark, TensorFlow, Koalas, Ray, Dask, etc.

Compute resources
 Apache Hadoop YARN, Kubernetes, Amazon Web Services, Slurm Workload Manager, etc.

We say a problem is *compute-bound* if the limiting factor is not the amount of data but rather the work we are doing on the data. *Memory-bound* problems are problems in which the computation is not the limiting factor; rather, the ability to store all the data in memory is the limiting factor. Some problems can be both compute-bound and memory-bound, as is often the case for large deep-learning problems.

Multi-core (think multi-threading) processing can help with compute-bound problems (up to the limit of the number of cores in a machine). Generally, multi-core processing is unable to help with memory-bound problems, as all Central Processing Units (CPUs) have similar access to the memory.[2]

Accelerated processing, including the use of specialized instruction sets or specialized hardware like Tensor Processing Units or Graphics Processing Units, is generally useful only for compute-bound problems. Sometimes using accelerated processing introduces memory-bound problems, as the amount of memory available to the accelerated computation can be smaller than the "main" system memory.

Multi-machine processing is important for both classes of problems. Since the number of cores you can get in a machine (affordably) is limited, even if a problem is "only" compute bound at certain scales, you will need to consider multi-machine processing. More commonly, memory-bound problems are a good fit for multi-machine scaling, as Dask can often split the data between the different machines.

Dask has both multi-core and multi-machine scaling, allowing you to scale your Python code as you see fit.

Much of Dask's power comes from the tools and libraries built on top of it, which fit into their parts of the data processing ecosystem (such as BlazingSQL). Your background and interest will naturally shape how you first view Dask, so in the following subsections, we'll briefly discuss how you can use Dask for different types of problems, as well as how it compares to some existing tools.

Big Data

Dask has better Python library integrations and lower overhead for tasks than many alternatives. Apache Spark (and its Python companion, PySpark) is one of the most popular tools for big data. Existing big data tools, such as PySpark, have more data sources and optimizers (like predicate push-down) but higher overhead per task. Dask's lower overhead is due mainly to the rest of the Python big data ecosystem being built primarily on top of the JVM. These tools have advanced features such as query optimizers, but with the cost of copying data between the JVM and Python.

Unlike many other traditional big data tools, such as Spark and Hadoop, Dask considers local mode a first-class citizen. The traditional big data ecosystem focuses on using the local mode for testing, but Dask focuses on good performance when running on a single node.

---

2 With the exception of non-uniform memory access (NUMA) systems.

Another significant cultural difference comes from packaging, with many projects in big data putting everything together (for example, Spark SQL, Spark Kubernetes, and so on are released together). Dask takes a more modular approach, with its components following their own development and release cadence. Dask's approach can iterate faster, at the cost of occasional incompatibilities between libraries.

Data Science

One of the most popular Python libraries in the data science ecosystem is pandas. Apache Spark (and its Python companion, PySpark) is also one of the most popular tools for distributed data science. It has support for both Python and JVM languages. Spark's first attempt at DataFrames more closely resembled SQL than what you may think of as DataFrames. While Spark has started to integrate pandas support with the Koalas project (*https://oreil.ly/VmU6O*), Dask's support of data science library APIs is best in class, in our opinion.[3] In addition to the pandas APIs, Dask supports scaling NumPy, scikit-learn, and other data science tools.

> Dask can be extended to support data types besides NumPy and pandas, and this is how GPU support is implemented with cuDF (*https://oreil.ly/m-K8W*).

Parallel to Distributed Python

Parallel computing refers to running multiple operations at the same time, and *distributed computing* carries this on to multiple operations on multiple machines. Parallel Python encompasses a wide variety of tools ranging from multi-processing to Celery.[4] Dask gives you the ability to specify an arbitrary graph of dependencies and execute them in parallel. Under the hood, this execution can either be backed by a single machine (with threads or processes) or be distributed across multiple workers.

---

3 Of course, opinions vary. See, for example, "Single Node Processing — Spark, Dask, Pandas, Modin, Koalas Vol. 1" (*https://oreil.ly/HBExc*), "Benchmark: Koalas (PySpark) and Dask" (*https://oreil.ly/PNZPm*), and "Spark vs. Dask vs. Ray" (*https://oreil.ly/eA28o*).

4 Celery, often used for background job management, is an asynchronous task queue that can also split up and distribute work. But it is at a lower level than Dask and does not have the same high-level conveniences as Dask.

Many big data tools have similar low-level task APIs, but they are internal and are not exposed for our use or protected against failures.

Dask Community Libraries

Dask's true power comes from the ecosystem built around it. Different libraries are built on top of Dask, giving you the ability to use multiple tools in the same framework. These community libraries are so powerful in part because of the combination of low-level and high-level APIs that are available for more than just first-party development.

Accelerated Python

You can accelerate Python in a few different ways, ranging from code generation (such as Numba) to libraries for special hardware such as NVidia's CUDA (and wrappers like cuDF), AMD's ROCm, and Intel's MKL.

Dask itself is not a library for accelerated Python, but you can use it in conjunction with accelerated Python tools. For ease of use, some community projects integrate acceleration tools, such as cuDF and dask-cuda, with Dask. When using accelerated Python tools with Dask, you'll need to be careful to structure your code to avoid serialization errors (see "Serialization and Pickling" on page 22).

Accelerated Python libraries tend to use more "native" memory structures, which are not as easily handled by pickle.

SQL engines

Dask itself does not have a SQL engine; however, FugueSQL (*https://oreil.ly/sBLQM*), Dask-SQL (*https://oreil.ly/ZMVD1*), and BlazingSQL (*https://oreil.ly/4gHru*) use Dask to provide a distributed SQL engine.[5] Dask-SQL uses the popular Apache Calcite project, which powers many other SQL engines. BlazingSQL extends Dask Data-Frames to support GPU operations. cuDF DataFrames have a slightly different representation. Apache Arrow makes it straightforward to convert a Dask DataFrame to cuDF and vice versa.

---

5 BlazingSQL is no longer maintained, though its concepts are interesting and may find life in another project.

Dask allows these different SQL engines to scale both memory- and compute-wise, handling larger data sizes than fit in memory on a single computer and processing rows on multiple computers. Dask also powers the important aggregation step of combining the results from the different machines into a cohesive view of the data.

 Dask-SQL can read data from parts of the Hadoop ecosystem that Dask cannot read from (e.g., Hive).

Workflow scheduling

Most organizations have the need for some kind of scheduled work, from programs that run at specific times (such as those that calculate end-of-day or end-of-month financials) to programs that run in response to events. These events can be things like data becoming available (such as after the daily financials are run) or a new email coming in, or they can be user triggered. In the simplest case the scheduled work can be a single program, but it is often more complex than that.

As mentioned previously, you can specify arbitrary graphs in Dask, and if you chose to, you could write your workflows using Dask itself. You can call system commands and parse their results, but just because you can do something doesn't mean it will be fun or simple.

The household name[6] for workflow scheduling in the big data ecosystem is Apache Airflow. While Airflow has a wonderful collection of operators, making it easy to express complex task types easily, it is notoriously difficult to scale.[7] Dask can be used to run Airflow tasks (*https://oreil.ly/Vw54J*). Alternatively, it can be used as a backend for other task scheduling systems like Prefect (*https://oreil.ly/9Xmvo*). Prefect aims to bring Airflow-like functionality to Dask with a large predefined task library. Since Prefect used Dask as an execution backend from the start, it has a tighter integration and lower overhead than Airflow on Dask.

---

6 Assuming a fairly nerdy household.

7 With one thousand tasks per hour taking substantial tuning and manual consideration; see "Scaling Airflow to 1000 Tasks/Hour" (*https://oreil.ly/tVbSf*).

Few tools cover all of the same areas, with the most similar tool being Ray. Dask and Ray both expose Python APIs, with underlying extensions when needed. There is a GitHub issue (*https://oreil.ly/cPJpW*) where the creators of both systems compare their similarities and differences. From a systems perspective, the biggest differences between Ray and Dask are handling state, fault tolerance, and centralized versus decentralized scheduling. Ray implements more of its logic in C++, which can have performance benefits but is also more difficult to read. From a user point of view, Dask has more of a data science focus, and Ray emphasizes distributed state and actor support. Dask can use Ray as a backend for scheduling.[8]

What Dask Is Not

While Dask is many things, it is not a magic wand you wave over your code to make it faster. There are places where Dask has largely compatible drop-in APIs, but misusing them can result in slower execution. Dask is not a code rewriting or just-in-time (JIT) tool; instead, Dask allows you to scale these tools to run on clusters. Dask focuses on Python and may not be the right tool for scaling languages not tightly integrated with Python (such as Go). Dask does not have built-in catalog support (e.g., Hive or Iceberg), so reading and writing data from tables stored with the catalogs can pose a challenge.

Conclusion

Dask is one of the possible options for scaling your analytical Python code. It covers various deployment options, from multiple cores on a single computer to data centers. Dask takes a modular approach compared to many other tools in similar spaces, which means that taking the time to understand the ecosystem and libraries around it is essential. The right choice to scale your software depends on your code and on the ecosystem, data consumers, and sources for your project. We hope we've convinced you that it's worth the time to play with Dask a bit, which you do in the next chapter.

---

8 Or, flipping the perspective, Ray is capable of using Dask to provide data science functionality.

## CHAPTER 2

Getting Started with Dask

We are so happy that you've decided to explore whether Dask is the system for you by trying it out. In this chapter, we will focus on getting started with Dask in its local mode. Using this, we'll explore a few more straightforward parallel computing tasks (including everyone's favorite, word count).[1]

Installing Dask Locally

Installing Dask locally is reasonably straightforward. If you want to begin running on multiple machines, doing so is often easier when you start with a conda environment (or virtualenv). This lets you figure out what packages you depend on by running `pip` `freeze` to make sure they're on all of the workers when it's time to scale.

While you can just run `pip` `install` `-U` `dask`, we prefer using a conda environment since it's easier to match the version of Python to that on a cluster, which allows us to connect a local machine to the cluster directly.[2] If you don't already have conda on your machine, Miniforge (*https://oreil.ly/qVDa7*) is a good and quick way to get conda installed across multiple platforms. The installation of Dask into a new conda environment is shown in Example 2-1.

---

1 Word count may be a somewhat tired example, but it is an important example, since it covers both work that can be done with minimal co-ordination (splitting up the text into words) and work requiring co-ordination between computers (summing the words).

2 There are downsides to deploying your Dask application in this way, as discussed in Chapter 12, but it can be an excellent debugging technique.

Example 2-1. Installing Dask into a new conda environment

```
conda create -n dask python=3.8.6  mamba -y
conda activate dask
mamba install --yes python==3.8.6 cytoolz dask==2021.7.0 numpy \
     pandas==1.3.0 beautifulsoup4 requests
```

Here we install a specific version of Dask rather than just the latest version. If you're planning to connect to a cluster later on, it will be useful to pick the same version of Dask as is installed on the cluster.

 You don't have to install Dask locally. There is a BinderHub example with Dask (*https://oreil.ly/EK5n5*) and distributed options, including one from the creators of Dask (*https://oreil.ly/3UEq-*), that you can use to run Dask, as well as other providers such as SaturnCloud (*https://oreil.ly/_6SyV*). That being said, we recommend having Dask installed locally even if you end up using one of these services.

Using Dask Docker Images

Another way to get Dask running locally is to use example Docker images (*https://oreil.ly/zCeHQ*) maintained by the Dask project. The benefit of this approach is that the same image can then be used in a distributed cluster, each node running the same Docker image locally, thus ensuring the compatibility of all the packages. Advanced users can use the Dask example Docker images as a base and add packages of their choice before committing changes and saving it as a new image (*https://oreil.ly/S1ms1*).

Hello Worlds

Now that you have Dask installed locally, it's time to try the versions of "Hello World" available through its various APIs. There are many different options for starting Dask. For now, you should use LocalCluster, as shown in Example 2-2.

Example 2-2. Using LocalCluster to start Dask

```
import dask
from dask.distributed import Client
client = Client() # Here we could specify a cluster, defaults to local mode
```

Task Hello World

One of the core building blocks of Dask is `dask.delayed`, which allows you to run functions in parallel. If you are running Dask on multiple machines, these functions can also be distributed (or spread out) on the different machines. When you wrap a function with `dask.delayed` and call it, you get back a "delayed" object representing the desired computation. When you created a delayed object, Dask is just making a note of what you might want it to do. As with a lazy teenager, you need to be explicit. You can force Dask to start computing the value with `dask.submit`, which produces a "future." You can use `dask.compute` both to start computing the delayed objects and futures and to return their values.[3]

Sleepy task

An easy way to see the performance difference is by writing an intentionally slow function, like `slow_task`, which calls `sleep`. Then you can compare the performance of Dask to "regular" Python by mapping the function over a few elements with and without `dask.delayed`, as shown in Example 2-3.

Example 2-3. Sleepy task

```
import timeit


def slow_task(x):
    import time
    time.sleep(2) # Do something sciency/business
    return x


things = range(10)

very_slow_result = map(slow_task, things)
slowish_result = map(dask.delayed(slow_task), things)

slow_time = timeit.timeit(lambda: list(very_slow_result), number=1)
fast_time = timeit.timeit(
    lambda: list(
        dask.compute(
            *slowish_result)),
    number=1)
print("In sequence {}, in parallel {}".format(slow_time, fast_time))
```

---

3 Provided they fit in memory.

When we run this example, we get In sequence 20.01662155520171, in parallel 6.259156636893749, which shows that Dask can run some of the tasks in parallel, but not all of them.[4]

Nested tasks

One of the neat things about dask.delayed is that you can launch tasks inside of other tasks.[5] A straightforward real-world example of this is a web crawler, with which, when you visit a web page, you want to fetch all of the links from that page, as shown in Example 2-4.

Example 2-4. Web crawler

```
@dask.delayed
def crawl(url, depth=0, maxdepth=1, maxlinks=4):
    links = []
    link_futures = []
    try:
        import requests
        from bs4 import BeautifulSoup
        f = requests.get(url)
        links += [(url, f.text)]
        if (depth > maxdepth):
            return links # base case
        soup = BeautifulSoup(f.text, 'html.parser')
        c = 0
        for link in soup.find_all('a'):
            if "href" in link:
                c = c + 1
                link_futures += crawl(link["href"],
                                      depth=(depth + 1),
                                      maxdepth=maxdepth)
                # Don't branch too much; we're still in local mode and the web is
                # big
                if c > maxlinks:
                    break
        for r in dask.compute(link_futures):
            links += r
        return links
    except requests.exceptions.InvalidSchema:
        return [] # Skip non-web links


dask.compute(crawl("http://holdenkarau.com/"))
```

---

4 When we run this on a cluster, we get worse performance, as there is overhead to distributing a task to a remote computer compared to the small delay.

5 This is very different from Apache Spark, where only the driver/head node can launch tasks.

In practice, some central co-ordination is still involved behind the scenes (including the scheduler), but the freedom to write your code in this nested way is quite powerful.

We cover other kinds of task dependencies in "Task Dependencies" on page 28.

Distributed Collections

In addition to the low-level task APIs, Dask also has distributed collections. These collections enable you to work with data that would be too large to fit on a single machine and to naturally distribute work on it, which is called *data parallelism*. Dask has both an unordered collection called a *bag*, and an ordered collection called an *array*. Dask arrays aim to implement some of the ndarray interface, whereas bags focus more on functional programming (e.g., things like map and filter). You can load Dask collections from files, take local collections and distribute them, or take the results of dask.delayed tasks and turn them into a collection.

In distributed collections, Dask splits the data up using partitions. Partitions are used to decrease the scheduling cost compared to operating on individual rows, which is covered in more detail in "Partitioning/Chunking Collections" on page 24.

Dask arrays

Dask arrays allow you to go beyond what can fit in memory, or even on disk, on a single computer. Many of the standard NumPy operations are supported out of the box, including aggregates such as average and standard deviation. The from_array function in Dask arrays converts a local array-like collection into a distributed collection. Example 2-5 shows how to create a distributed array from a local one and then compute the average.

Example 2-5. Creating a distributed array and computing the average

```
import dask.array as da
distributed_array = da.from_array(list(range(0, 1000)))
avg = dask.compute(da.average(distributed_array))
```

As with all distributed collections, what is expensive on a Dask array is not the same as what is expensive on a local array. In the next chapter you'll learn a bit more about how Dask arrays are implemented and hopefully gain a better intuition around their performance.

Creating a distributed collection from a local collection uses the two fundamental building blocks of distributed computing, called the *scatter-gather pattern*. While the originating dataset must be from a local computer, fitting into a single machine, this already expands the number of processors you have at your disposal, as well as the intermediate memory you can utilize, enabling you to better exploit modern cloud infrastructure and scale. A practical use case would be a distributed web crawler, where the list of seed URLs to crawl might be a small dataset, but the memory you need to hold while crawling might be an order of magnitude larger, requiring distributed computing.

Dask bags and a word count

Dask bags implement more of the functional programming interfaces than Dask arrays. The "Hello World" of big data is word count, which is easier to implement with functional programming interfaces. Since you've already made a crawler function, you can turn its output into a Dask bag using the from_delayed function in Example 2-6.

Example 2-6. Turning the crawler function's output into a Dask bag

```
import dask.bag as db
githubs = [
    "https://github.com/scalingpythonml/scalingpythonml",
    "https://github.com/dask/distributed"]
initial_bag = db.from_delayed(map(crawl, githubs))
```

Now that you have a Dask bag collection, you can build everyone's favorite word count example on top of it. The first step is to turn your bag of text into a bag of words, which you do by using map (see Example 2-7). Once you have the bag of words, you can either use Dask's built-in frequency method (see Example 2-8) or write your own frequency method using functional transformations (see Example 2-9).

Example 2-7. Turning a bag of text into a bag of words

```
words_bag = initial_bag.map(
    lambda url_contents: url_contents[1].split(" ")).flatten()
```

Example 2-8. Using Dask's built-in frequency method

```
dask.compute(words_bag.frequencies())
```

Example 2-9. Using functional transformations to write a custom `frequency` method

```
def make_word_tuple(w):
    return (w, 1)


def get_word(word_count):
    return word_count[0]


def sum_word_counts(wc1, wc2):
    return (wc1[0], wc1[1] + wc2[1])


word_count = words_bag.map(make_word_tuple).foldby(get_word, sum_word_counts)
```

On Dask bags, `foldby`, `frequency`, and many other reductions return a single partition bag, meaning the data after reduction needs to fit in a single computer. Dask DataFrames handle reductions differently and don't have that same restriction.

Dask DataFrame (Pandas/What People Wish Big Data Was)

Pandas is one of the most popular Python data libraries, and Dask has a DataFrame library that implements much of the pandas API. Thanks to Python's duck-typing, you can often use Dask's distributed DataFrame library in place of pandas. Not all of the API will work exactly the same, and some parts are not implemented, so be sure you have good test coverage.

Your intuition around what's slow and fast with pandas does not carry over. We will explore this more in "Dask DataFrames" on page 25.

To illustrate how you can use Dask DataFrame, we'll rework Examples 2-6 through 2-8 to use it. As with Dask's other collections, you can create DataFrames from local collections, futures, or distributed files. Since you've already made a crawler function, you can turn its output into a Dask bag using the `from_delayed` function from Example 2-6. Instead of using `map` and `foldby`, you can use pandas APIs such as `explode` and `value_counts`, as shown in Example 2-10.

Example 2-10. DataFrame word count

```
import dask.dataframe as dd


@dask.delayed
def crawl_to_df(url, depth=0, maxdepth=1, maxlinks=4):
    import pandas as pd
    crawled = crawl(url, depth=depth, maxdepth=maxdepth, maxlinks=maxlinks)
    return pd.DataFrame(crawled.compute(), columns=[
                        "url", "text"]).set_index("url")


delayed_dfs = map(crawl_to_df, githubs)
initial_df = dd.from_delayed(delayed_dfs)
wc_df = initial_df.text.str.split().explode().value_counts()

dask.compute(wc_df)
```

Conclusion

In this chapter you got Dask working on your local machine, as well as had a tour of the different "Hello World" (or getting started) examples with most of Dask's different built-in libraries. Subsequent chapters will dive into these different tools in more detail.

Now that you've got Dask working on your local machine, you might want to jump on over to Chapter 12 and look at the different deployment mechanisms. For the most part, you can run the examples in local mode, albeit sometimes a little slower or at a smaller scale. However, the next chapter will look at the core concepts of Dask, and one of the upcoming examples emphasizes the benefits of having Dask running on multiple machines and is also generally easier to explore on a cluster. If you don't have a cluster available, you may wish to set up a simulated one using something like MicroK8s (*https://microk8s.io*).

## CHAPTER 3

How Dask Works: The Basics

Now that you've run your first few tasks with Dask, it's time to learn a little bit about what's happening behind the scenes. Depending on whether you are using Dask locally or in a distributed fashion, the behavior can be a little different. While Dask does a good job of abstracting away many of the details of running on multiple threads or servers, having a solid grasp of how Dask is working will help you better decide both how and when to use it.

To be familiar with Dask, you need to understand:

- The deployment framework that Dask is able to run on, and its strengths and weaknesses
- The types of data that Dask is able to read, and how you can interact with the data types in Dask
- The computational pattern of Dask, and how to turn your ideas into Dask code
- How to monitor and troubleshoot

In this chapter, we will introduce each of these concepts, and we will expand upon them in the rest of the book.

Execution Backends

Dask has many different execution backends, but we find it easiest to think about them in two groups, local and distributed. With local backends, you are limited in scale to what a single computer can handle. Local backends also have advantages like the avoidance of network overhead, simpler library management, and a lower dollar cost.[1] Dask's distributed backend has many options for deployment, from cluster managers such as Kubernetes to job queue–like systems.

Local Backends

Dask's three local backends are single-process, multi-threaded, and multi-process. The single-process backend has no parallelism and is mostly useful for validating that a problem is caused by concurrency. Multi-threaded and multi-process backends are ideal for problems in which the data is small or the cost of copying it would be higher than computation time.

 If you don't configure a specific local backend, Dask will pick the backend based on the library you are working with.

The local multi-threaded scheduler is able to avoid having to serialize data and interprocess communication costs. The multi-threaded backend is suited for tasks in which the majority of the computation is happening in native code, outside of Python. This is the case for many numeric libraries, such as pandas and NumPy. If that is the case for you, you can configure Dask to use multi-threading, as shown in Example 3-1.

Example 3-1. Configuring Dask to use multi-threading

```
dask.config.set(scheduler='threads')
```

The local multi-process backend, shown in Example 3-2, has some additional overhead over multi-threaded, although it can be decreased on Unix and Unix-like systems.[2] The multi-process backend is able to avoid Python's global interpreter lock by launching separate processes. Launching a new process is more expensive than a new thread, and Dask needs to serialize data that moves between processes.[3]

Example 3-2. Configuring Dask to use the multi-process backend

```
dask.config.set(scheduler='processes')
```

---

1 Unless you work for a cloud provider and computers are close to free. If you do work for a cloud provider, please send us cloud credits.

2 Including OS X and Linux.

3 This also involves having to store a second copy of any object that is in the driver thread and then used in a worker. Since Dask shards its collections, this doesn't generally blow up as quickly as it would with normal multi-processing.

If you are running on a Unix system, you can use the *forkserver*, shown in Example 3-3, which will reduce the overhead of starting each Python interpreter (*https://oreil.ly/U9voe*). Using the forkserver will not reduce the communication overhead.

Example 3-3. Configuring Dask to use the multi-process forkserver

```
dask.config.set({"multiprocessing.context": "forkserver",
                 "scheduler": "processes"})
```

This optimization is generally not available on Windows.

Dask's local backends are designed for performance rather than for testing that your code will work on a distributed scheduler. To test that your code will run remotely, you should use Dask's distributed scheduler with a LocalCluster instead.

Distributed (Dask Client and Scheduler)

While Dask can work well locally, its true power comes with the distributed scheduler, with which you can scale your problem to multiple machines. Since there are physical and financial limits to how much computing power, storage, and memory can be put into one machine, using multiple machines is often the most cost-efficient solution (and it is sometimes the only solution). Distributed computing is not without its drawbacks; as Leslie Lamport famously said, "A distributed system is one in which the failure of a computer you didn't even know existed can render your own computer unusable." While Dask does much to limit these failures (see "Fault Tolerance" on page 32), you accept some increase in complexity when moving to a distributed system.

Dask has one distributed scheduler backend, and it talks to many different types of clusters, including a LocalCluster. Each type of cluster is supported in its own library, which schedules the scheduler[4] that the Dask client then connects to. Using the distributed abstraction dask.distributed gives you portability between any types of cluster you may be using at the moment, including local. If you don't use dask.distributed, Dask can still run perfectly well on a local computer, in which case you are using a default single-machine scheduler provided in the Dask library.

The Dask client is your entry point into the Dask distributed scheduler. In this chapter, we will be using Dask with a Kubernetes cluster; if you have another type of cluster or want details, please see Chapter 12.

---

4 Say that five times fast.

Auto-scaling

With auto-scaling, Dask can increase or decrease the computers/resources being used, based on the tasks you have asked it to run.[5] For example, if you have a program that computes complex aggregations using many computers but then mostly operates on the aggregated data, the number of computers you need could decrease by a large amount post-aggregation. Many workloads, including machine learning, do not need the same amount of resources/computers the entire time.

Some of Dask's cluster backends, including Kubernetes, support auto-scaling, which Dask calls *adaptive deployments*. Auto-scaling is useful mostly in situations of shared cluster resources, or when running on cloud providers where the underlying resources are paid for by the hour.

Important limitations with the Dask client

Dask's client is not fault tolerant, so while Dask can handle the failures of its workers, if the connection between the client and the scheduler is broken, your application will fail. A common workaround for this is scheduling the client within the same environment as the scheduler, although this does somewhat reduce the usefulness of having the client and scheduler as separate components.

Libraries and dependencies in distributed clusters

Part of why Dask is so powerful is the Python ecosystem that it is in. While Dask will pickle, or serialize (see "Serialization and Pickling" on page 22), and send our code to the workers, this doesn't include the libraries we use.[6] To take advantage of that ecosystem, you need to be able to use additional libraries. During the exploration phase, it is common to install packages at runtime as you discover that you need them.

The `PipInstall` worker plug-in takes a list of packages and installs them at runtime on all of the workers. Looking back at Example 2-4, to install bs4 you would call `distributed.diagnostics.plugin.PipInstall(["bs4"])`. Any new workers that are launched by Dask then need to wait for the package to be installed. The `Pip Install` plug-in is ideal for quick prototyping when you are discovering which packages you need. You can think of `PipInstall` as the replacement for `!pip install` in a notebook over having a virtualenv.

---

5 As in many real-world situations, it's easier to grow and harder to shrink the number of Dask nodes

6 Automatically picking up and shipping the libraries would be very hard and also slow, although it can be done under certain circumstances.

To avoid the slowness of having to install packages each time a new worker is launched, you should try to pre-install your libraries. Each cluster manager (e.g., YARN, Kubernetes, Coiled, Saturn, etc.) has its own methods for managing dependencies. This can happen at runtime or at setup where the packages are pre-installed. The specifics for the different cluster managers are covered in Chapter 12.

With Kubernetes, for example, the default startup script checks for the presence of some key environment variables (EXTRA_APT_PACKAGES, EXTRA_CONDA_PACKAGES, and EXTRA_PIP_PACKAGES), which, in conjunction with customized worker specs, can be used to add dependencies at runtime. Some of them, like Coiled and Kubernetes, allow for adding dependencies when building an image for our workers. Others, like YARN, use preallocated conda/virtual environment packing.

 It is very important to have the same versions of Python and libraries installed on all of the workers and your client. Different versions of libraries can lead to outright failures or subtler data correctness issues.

Dask's Diagnostics User Interface

One of your first stops in understanding what your program is doing should be Dask's Diagnostics UI. The UI allows you to see what Dask is executing, the number of worker threads/processes/computers, memory utilization information, and much more. If you are running Dask locally, you will likely find the UI at *http://localhost:8787*.

If you're using the Dask client to connect to a cluster, the UI will be running on the scheduler node. You can get the link to the dashboard from client.dashboard_link.

 For remote notebook users, the hostname of the scheduler node may not be reachable directly from your computer. One option is to use the Jupyter proxy; for example, one might go to http://jupyter.example.com/user/username/proxy/dask-head-4c81d51e-3.jhub:8787/status to access the endpoint dask-head-4c81d51e-3.jhub:8787/status.

Figure 3-1 shows the Dask UI during the running of the examples in this chapter.

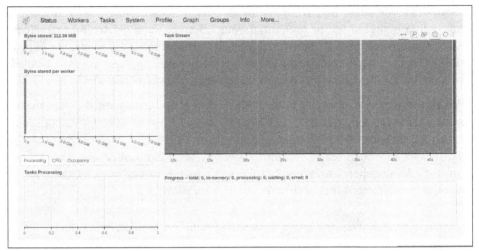

Figure 3-1. The Dask UI (digital, color version: https://oreil.ly/PuWRN)

The UI allows you to see what Dask is doing and what's being stored on the workers and to explore the execution graph. We will revisit the execution graph in "visualize" on page 28.

Serialization and Pickling

Distributed and parallel systems depend on serialization, sometimes called *pickling* in Python, to share data and functions/code between processes. Dask uses a mixture of serialization techniques to match the use case and provides hooks to extend by class when the defaults don't meet your needs.

 We most often think of serialization when it fails (with an error), but equally important can be situations where we end up serializing more data than we need—or when the amount of data that needs to be transferred is so large that distributing the work is no longer beneficial.

Cloudpickle serializes the functions and the generic Python types in Dask. Most Python code doesn't depend on serializing functions, but cluster computing often does. Cloudpickle is a project designed for cluster computing and is able to serialize and deserialize more functions than Python's built-in pickle.

Dask has its own ability to extend serialization, but the registry methods are not automatically sent to the workers, and it's not always used.[7]

Dask has built-in special handling for NumPy arrays, sparse, and cuPY. These serializations tend to be more space efficient than the default serializers. When you make a class that contains one of these types and does not require any special initialization, you should call `register_generic(YourClass)` from `dask.distributed.protocol` to take advantage of Dask's special handling.

If you have a class that is not serializable, as in Example 3-4, you can wrap it to add serialization functions to it, as shown in Example 3-5.

Example 3-4. Dask fails to serialize

```
class ConnectionClass:
    def __init__(self, host, port):
        import socket
        self.socket = socket.socket(socket.AF_INET, socket.SOCK_STREAM)
        self.socket.connect((host, port))


@dask.delayed
def bad_fun(x):
    return ConnectionClass("www.scalingpythonml.com", 80)


# Fails to serialize
if False:
    dask.compute(bad_fun(1))
```

Example 3-5. Custom serialization

```
class SerConnectionClass:
    def __init__(self, conn):
        import socket
        self.conn = conn

    def __getstate__(self):
        state_dict = {
            "host": self.conn.socket.getpeername()[0],
            "port": self.conn.socket.getpeername()[1]}
        return state_dict
```

---

7 See Dask distributed GitHub issues 5561 (*https://oreil.ly/DmFxp*) and 2953 (*https://oreil.ly/RxzGS*).

```
def __setsate__(self, state):
    self.conn = ConnectionClass(state["host"], state["port"])
```

If you control the original class, you can also directly add the getstate/setstate methods instead of wrapping it.

 Dask automatically attempts to compress serialized data, which generally improves performance. You can disable this by setting distributed.comm.compression to None.

Partitioning/Chunking Collections

Partitioning gives you the ability to control the number of tasks used to process your data. If you have billions of rows, using one task for each row would mean you spend more time scheduling the tasks than doing the work itself. Understanding partitioning is key to being able to make the most efficient use of Dask.

Dask uses slightly different terminology for partitioning in each of its collections. In Dask, partitioning impacts how data is located on your cluster, and the right partitioning for your problem can make order-of-magnitude improvements. Partitioning has a few different aspects, like the size of each partition, the number of partitions, and optional properties such as partition key and sorted versus unsorted.

The number and size of partitions are closely related and impact the maximum parallelism. Partitions that are too small or too great in number mean that Dask will spend more time scheduling the tasks than running them. A general sweet spot for partition size is around 100 MB to 1 GB, but if your computation per element is very expensive, smaller partition sizes can perform better.

Ideally, your partitions should be similar in size to avoid stragglers. A situation in which you've got partitions of different sizes is called *skewed*. There are many different sources of skew, ranging from input file sizes to key skew (when keyed). When your data gets too skewed, you will need to repartition the data.

 The Dask UI is a great place to see if you might have stragglers.

Dask Arrays

Dask arrays' partitions are called *chunks* and represent the number of elements. Although Dask always knows the number of chunks, when you apply a filter or load

---

data, Dask is unaware of the size of each chunk. Indexing or slicing a Dask array requires that Dask know the chunk sizes so it can find the chunk(s) with the desired elements. Depending on how your Dask array was created, Dask may or may not know the size of each chunk. We talk about this more in Chapter 5. If you want to index into an array where Dask does not know the chunk sizes, you will need to first call `compute_chunk_sizes()` on the array. When creating a Dask array from a local collection, you can specify the target chunk size, as shown in Example 3-6.

Example 3-6. Custom array chunk size

```
distributed_array = da.from_array(list(range(0, 10000)), chunks=10)
```

Partitions/chunking doesn't have to be static, and the `rechunk` function allows you to change the chunk size of a Dask array.

Dask Bags

Dask bags' partitions are called *partitions*. Unlike with Dask arrays, since Dask bags do not support indexing, Dask does not track the number of elements in each partition. When you use `scatter`, Dask will try to partition the data as well as possible, but subsequent iterations can change the number of elements inside each partition. Similar to Dask arrays, when creating from a local collection, you can specify the number of partitions of a bag, except the parameter is called `npartitions` instead of `chunks`.

You can change the number of partitions in a bag by calling `repartition` with either `npartitions` (for a fixed number of partitions) or `partition_size` (for a target size of each partition). Specifying `partition_size` is more expensive since Dask needs to do some extra computation to determine what the matching number of partitions would be.

You can think of data as keyed when there is an index or when the data can be looked up by a value, such as in a hashtable. While bags implement keyed operations like `groupBy`, where values with the same key are combined, their partitioning does not have any idea of key and instead keyed operations always operate on all partitions.[8]

Dask DataFrames

DataFrames have the most options for partitioning. DataFrames can have partitions of different sizes, as well as known or unknown partitioning. With unknown partitioning, the data is distributed, but Dask is unable to determine which partition holds

---

8 Coming from databases, you can think of this as a "full-scan" or "full-shuffle" for Spark folks with `groupBy`.

a particular key. Unknown partitioning happens often, as any operation that could change the value of a key results in unknown partitioning. The known_divisions property on a DataFrame allows you to see whether Dask knows the partitioning, and the index property shows the splits used and the column.

If a DataFrame has the right partitioning, operations like groupBy, which would normally involve a lot of internode communication, can be executed with less communication. Accessing rows by ID requires that the DataFrame is partitioned on that key. If you want to change the column that your DataFrame is partitioned on, you can call set_index to change the index. Setting the index, like all the repartitioning operations, involves copying the data between workers, known as a *shuffle*.

The "right" partitioner for a dataset depends on not only the data but also your operations.

Shuffles

Shuffling refers to transferring data between different workers to repartition the data. Shuffling can be the result of an explicit operation, like calling repartition, or an implicit one, like grouping data together by key or performing an aggregation. Shuffles tend to be relatively expensive, so it's useful to minimize how often they are needed and also to reduce the amount of data they move.

The most straightforward case to understand shuffles is when you explicitly ask Dask to repartition your data. In those cases you generally see many-to-many worker communication, with the majority of the data needing to be moved over the network. This is naturally more expensive than situations in which data is able to be processed locally, as the network is much slower than RAM.

Another important way that you can trigger shuffles is implicitly through a reduction/aggregation. In such cases, if parts of the reduction or aggregation can be applied prior to moving the data around, Dask is able to transfer less data over the network, making for a faster shuffle.

Sometimes you'll see things referred to as *map-side* and *reduce-side*; this just means before and after the shuffle.

We'll explore more about how to minimize the impact of shuffles in the next two chapters, where we introduce aggregations.

Partitions During Load

So far you've seen how to control partitions when creating from a local collection, as well as how to change the partitioning of an existing distributed collection. Partitioning during the creation of a collection from delayed tasks is generally 1:1, with each delayed task being its own partition. When loading data from files, partitioning becomes a bit more complicated, involving file layout and compression. Generally speaking, it is good practice to look at the partitioning of data you have loaded by calling npartitions for bags, chunks for arrays, or index for DataFrames.

Tasks, Graphs, and Lazy Evaluation

Tasks are the building blocks that Dask uses to implement dask.delayed, futures, and operations on Dask's collections. Each task represents a small piece of computation that Dask cannot break down any further. Tasks are often fine-grained, and when computing a result Dask will try to combine multiple tasks into a single execution.

Lazy Evaluation

Most of Dask is lazily evaluated, with the exception of Dask futures. Lazy evaluation shifts the responsibility for combining computations from you to the scheduler. This means that Dask will, when it makes sense, combine multiple function calls. Not only that, but if only some parts of a structure are needed, Dask is sometimes able to optimize by evaluating just the relevant parts (like head or tail calls).[9] Implementing lazy evaluation requires Dask to construct a task graph. This task graph is also reused for fault tolerance.

Unlike most of Dask, futures are eagerly evaluated, which limits the optimizations available when chaining them together, as the scheduler has a less complete view of the world when it starts executing the first future. Futures still create task graphs, and you can verify this by visualizing them in the next section.

Unlike the rest of Dask, futures are eagerly evaluated, which limits the optimizations available when chaining them together, as the scheduler has a less complete view of the world when it starts executing the first future. Futures still create task graphs, and you can verify this by visualizing them, as we'll see in the next section.

---

9 When Dask can optimize evaluation here is complicated, but remember that a task is the fundamental unit of computation and Dask cannot break down compute any further inside the task. So a DataFrame created from many individual tasks that you call head on is a great candidate for Dask to optimize, but for a single task making a large DataFrame, Dask is unable to break "inside."

Task Dependencies

In addition to nested tasks, as seen in "Nested tasks" on page 12, you can also use a dask.delayed object as input to another delayed computation (see Example 3-7), and Dask's submit/compute function will construct a task graph for you.

Example 3-7. Task dependencies

```
@dask.delayed()
def string_magic(x, y):
    lower_x = x.lower()
    lower_y = y.lower()
    return (lower_x in lower_y) or (lower_y in lower_x)


@dask.delayed()
def gen(x):
    return x


f = gen("hello world")
compute = string_magic(f, f)
```

Now when you go to compute the final combined value, Dask will compute all of the other values that are needed for the final function using its implicit task graph.

 You don't need to pass around real values. For example, if one function updates a database and you want to run another function after that, you can use it as a parameter even if you don't actually need its Python return value.

By passing delayed objects into other delayed function calls, you allow Dask to re-use shared nodes in the task graph and potentially reduce network overhead.

visualize

Visualizing the task graph is an excellent tool for you to use while learning about task graphs and debugging in the future. The visualize function is defined both in the Dask library and on all Dask objects. Instead of calling .visualize separately on multiple objects, you should call dask.visualize with the list of objects you are planning to compute to see how Dask combines the task graph.

You should try this out now by visualizing Examples 2-6 through 2-9. When you call dask.visualize on words_bag.frequencies(), you should get a result that looks something like Figure 3-2.

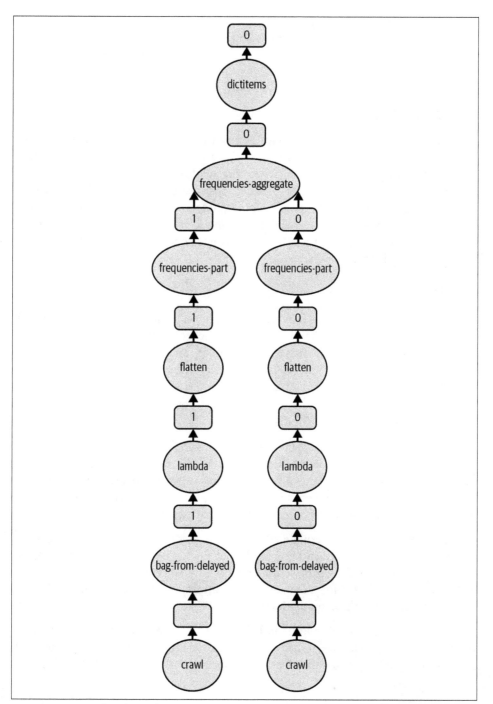

Figure 3-2. Visualized word count task graph (redrawn output)

The Dask UI also shows visualized representations of the task graph, without the need to modify your code.

Intermediate Task Results

Intermediate task results are generally removed as soon as the dependent task has started to execute. This can be less than optimal when we need to perform multiple computations on the same piece of data. One solution to this is combining all our execution together into one call to dask.compute, so that Dask is able to keep the data around as needed. This breaks down in both the interactive case, where we don't know in advance what our computation is going to be, and iterative cases. In those cases, some form of caching or persistence can be beneficial. You will learn about how to apply caching later in this chapter.

Task Sizing

Dask uses a centralized scheduler, which is a common technique for many systems. It does mean, however, that while the general task scheduling overhead is 1 ms, as the number of tasks in a system increases the scheduler can become a bottleneck, and the overhead can grow. Counterintuitively, this means that as our system grows we may benefit from larger, coarser-grained tasks.

When Task Graphs Get Too Large

Sometimes the task graph itself can become too much for Dask to handle. This issue can show up as an out-of-memory exception on the client or scheduler or, more commonly, as jobs that slow down with iterations. Most frequently this occurs with recursive algorithms. One common example of a situation in which the graph can become too expensive to keep is distributed alternating least squares.

The first step when encountering a situation with a too-large task graph is to see if you can reduce the parallelism by using larger chunks of work or by switching the algorithm. For example, if we think of Fibonacci numbers computed with recursion, a better option would be using a dynamic programming or memoized solution instead of trying to distribute the computation task with Dask.

If you have an iterative algorithm, and there isn't a better way to accomplish what you want, you can help Dask out by periodically writing out the intermediate work and re-loading it.[10] By doing this, Dask does not have to keep track of all of the steps

---

10 You could also collect and scatter if the dataset is small enough.

involved in creating the data, but instead just needs to remember where the data is. The next two chapters will look at how to write and load data efficiently for these and other purposes.

 In Spark the equivalent idea is expressed as *checkpointing*.

Combining Computation

To take the most advantage of Dask's graph optimization, it's important to submit your work in larger batches. First off, when you're blocking on the result with dask.compute, small batches can limit the parallelism. If you have a shared parent—say, two results on the same data—submitting the computations together allows Dask to share the computation of the underlying data. You can verify whether Dask is able to share a common node by calling visualize on your list of tasks (e.g., if you take Examples 2-8 and 2-9 and visualize both the tasks together, you'll see the shared node in Figure 3-2).

Sometimes you can't submit the computations together, but you still know that you want to reuse some data. In those cases you should explore persistence.

Persist, Caching, and Memoization

Persistence allows you to keep specified Dask collections in memory on the cluster. To persist a collection for future reuse, just call dask.persist on the collection. If you choose persistence, you will be responsible for telling Dask when you are done with a distributed collection. Unlike Spark, Dask does not have an easy unpersist equivalent; instead, you need to release the underlying futures for each partition as shown in Example 3-8.

Example 3-8. Manual persistence and memory management with Dask

```
df.persist
# You do a bunch of things on DF

# I'm done!
from distributed.client import futures_of
list(map(lambda x: x.release(), futures_of(df)))
```

A common mistake is to persist and cache things that are used only once or are inexpensive to compute.

Dask's local mode has a best-effort caching system based on cachey. Since this only works in local mode, we won't go into the details, but if you are running in local mode, you can take a look at the local cache documentation (*https://oreil.ly/VFSVQ*).

Dask does not raise an error when you attempt to use Dask caching in a distributed fashion; it just won't work. So when migrating code from local to distributed, make sure to check for usage of Dask's local caching.

Fault Tolerance

In distributed systems like Dask, *fault tolerance* generally refers to how a system handles computer, network, or program failures. Fault tolerance becomes increasingly important the more computers you use. When you are using Dask on a single computer, the concept of fault tolerance is less important, since if your one computer fails, there is nothing to recover. However, when you have hundreds of machines, the odds of a machine failing go up. Dask's task graph is used to provide its fault tolerance.[11] There are many different kinds of failures in a distributed system, but thankfully many of them can be handled in the same way.

Dask automatically retries tasks when the scheduler loses connection to the worker. This retry is accomplished by using the same graph of computation Dask uses for lazy evaluation.

The Dask client is *not* fault tolerant to network issues connecting to the scheduler. One mitigation technique you can use is to run your client in the same network as the scheduler.

Machine failure is a fact of life with distributed systems. When a worker fails, Dask will treat it in the same way as a network failure, retrying any necessary tasks. However, Dask cannot recover from failures of the scheduler of your client code.[12]

---

11 The same technique used in Spark.

12 This is common for most systems like this. Spark does have limited ability to recover from head node failure, but it has many restrictions and is not frequently used.

This makes it important that, when you are running in a shared environment, you run your client and scheduler nodes at a high priority to avoid preemption.

Dask automatically retries software failures that exit or crash the worker. Much like machine failure, from Dask's point of view a worker exiting and a network failing look the same.

IOError and OSError exceptions are the only two classes of exceptions Dask will retry. If your worker process raises one of these errors, the exception is pickled and transferred over to the scheduler. Dask's scheduler then retries the task. If your code encounters an IOError that should not be retried (e.g., a web page doesn't exist), you'll need to wrap it in another exception to keep Dask from retrying it.

Since Dask retries failed computation, it's important to be careful with side effects or changing values. For example, if you have a Dask bag of transactions and were to update a database as part of a map, Dask might re-execute some of the operations on that bag multiple times, resulting in the update to the database happening more than once. If we think of a withdrawal from an ATM, we can see how this would result in some unhappy customers and incorrect data. Instead, if you need to mutate small bits of data, you can bring them back to a local collection.

If your program encounters any other exceptions, Dask will return the exception to your main thread.[13]

Conclusion

After this chapter you should have a good grasp of how Dask is able to scale your Python code. You should now understand the basics of partitioning, why this matters, task sizing, and Dask's approach to fault tolerance. This will hopefully set you up well for deciding when to apply Dask, and for the next few chapters, where we do a deeper dive into Dask's collection libraries. In the next chapter we'll focus on Dask's DataFrames, as they are the most full-featured of Dask's distributed collections.

---

13 For those migrating from Spark, this retry behavior is different. Spark will retry most exceptions, whereas Dask will only retry errors resulting in a worker exiting, or an IOError or OSError.

## CHAPTER 4

Dask DataFrame

Pandas DataFrames, while popular, quickly run into memory constraints as data sizes grow, since they store the entirety of the data in memory. Pandas DataFrames have a robust API for all kinds of data manipulation and are frequently the starting point for many analytics and machine learning projects. While pandas itself does not have machine learning built in, data scientists often use it as part of data and feature preparation during the exploratory phase of new projects. As such, scaling pandas DataFrames to be able to handle large datasets is of vital importance to many data scientists. Most data scientists are already familiar with the pandas libraries, and Dask's DataFrame implements much of the pandas API while adding the ability to scale.

Dask is one of the first to implement a usable subset of the pandas APIs, but other projects such as Spark have added their approaches. This chapter assumes you have a good understanding of the pandas DataFrame APIs; if not, you should check out *Python for Data Analysis*.

You can often use Dask DataFrames as a replacement for pandas DataFrames with minor changes, thanks to duck-typing. However, this approach can have performance drawbacks, and some functions are not present. These drawbacks come from the distributed parallel nature of Dask, which adds communication costs for certain types of operations. In this chapter, you will learn how to minimize these performance drawbacks and work around any missing functionality.

Dask DataFrames require that your data and your computation are well suited to pandas DataFrames. Dask has bags for unstructured data, arrays for array-structured data, the Dask delayed interface for arbitrary functions, and actors for stateful operations. If even at a small scale you wouldn't consider using pandas for your problem, Dask DataFrames are probably not the right solution.

How Dask DataFrames Are Built

Dask DataFrames build on top of pandas DataFrames. Each partition is stored as a pandas DataFrame.[1] Using pandas DataFrames for the partitions simplifies the implementation of much of the APIs. This is especially true for row-based operations, where Dask passes the function call down to each pandas DataFrame.

Most of the distributed components of Dask DataFrames use the three core building blocks `map_partitions`, `reduction`, and `rolling`. You mostly won't need to call these functions directly; you will use higher-level APIs instead. But understanding these functions and how they work is important to understanding how Dask works. `shuffle` is a critical building block of distributed DataFrames for reorganizing your data. Unlike the other building blocks, you may use it directly more frequently, as Dask is unable to abstract away partitioning.

Loading and Writing

Data analytics is only as valuable as the data it has access to, and our insights are helpful only if they result in action. Since not all of our data is in Dask, it's essential to read and write data from the rest of the world. So far, the examples in this book have mainly used local collections, but you have many more options.

Dask supports reading and writing many standard file formats and filesystems. These formats include CSV, HDF, fixed-width, Parquet, and ORC. Dask supports many of the standard distributed filesystems, from HDFS to S3, and reading from regular filesystems.

Most important for Dask, distributed filesystems allow multiple computers to read and write to the same set of files. Distributed filesystems often store data on multiple computers, which allows for storing more data than a single computer can hold. Often, but not always, distributed filesystems are also fault tolerant (which they achieve through replication). Distributed filesystems can have important performance differences from what you are used to working with, so it's important to skim the user documentation for the filesystems you are using. Some things to look for are block sizes (you often don't want to write files smaller than these, as the rest is wasted space), latency, and consistency guarantees.

---

1 See "Partitioning/Chunking Collections" on page 24 for a review of partitioning.

Reading from regular local files can be complicated in Dask, as the files need to exist on all workers. If a file exists only on the head node, consider copying it to a distributed filesystem like S3 or NFS, or load it locally and use Dask's `client.scatter` function to distribute the data if it's small enough. Sufficiently small files *may* be a sign that you don't yet need Dask, unless the processing on them is complex or slow.

Formats

Dask's DataFrame loading and writing functions start with `to_` or `read_` as the prefixes. Each format has its own configuration, but in general, the first positional argument is the location of the data to be read. The location can be a wildcard path of files (e.g., *s3://test-bucket/magic/**), a list of files, or a regular file location.

Wildcard paths work only with filesystems that support directory listing. For example, they do not work on HTTP.

When loading data, having the right number of partitions will speed up all of your operations. Sometimes it's not possible to load the data with the right number of partitions, and in those cases you can repartition your data after the load. As discussed, more partitions allow for more parallelism but have a non-zero overhead. The different formats have slightly different ways to control this. HDF takes `chunksize`, indicating the number of rows per partition. Parquet also takes `split_row_groups`, which takes an integer of the desired logical partitioning out of the Parquet file, and Dask will split the whole set into those chunks, or less. If not given, the default behavior is for each partition to correspond to a Parquet file. The text-based formats (CSV, fixed-width, etc.) take a `blocksize` parameter with the same meaning as Parquet's `chunksize` but a maximum value of 64 MB. You can verify this by loading a dataset and seeing the number of tasks and partitions increase with smaller target sizes, as in Example 4-1.

Example 4-1. Dask DataFrame loading CSV with 1 KB chunks

```
many_chunks = dd.read_csv(url, blocksize="1kb")
many_chunks.index
```

Loading CSV and JSON files can be more complicated than Parquet, and other self-describing data types don't have any schema information encoded. Dask DataFrames need to know the types of the different columns to serialize the data correctly. By default, Dask will automatically look at the first few records and guess the data types for each column. This process is known as schema inference, and it can be quite slow.

Unfortunately, schema inference does not always work. For example, if you try to load the UK's gender pay gap disparity data from *https://gender-pay-gap .service.gov.uk/viewing/download-data/2021*, when you access the data, as in Example 4-2, you will get an error of "Mismatched dtypes found in `pd.read_csv/ pd.read_table`." When Dask's column type inference is incorrect, you can override it (per column) by specifying the `dtype` parameter, as shown in Example 4-3.

Example 4-2. Dask DataFrame loading CSV, depending entirely on inference

```
df = dd.read_csv(
    "https://gender-pay-gap.service.gov.uk/viewing/download-data/2021")
```

Example 4-3. Dask DataFrame loading CSV and specifying data type

```
df = dd.read_csv(
    "https://gender-pay-gap.service.gov.uk/viewing/download-data/2021",
    dtype={'CompanyNumber': 'str', 'DiffMeanHourlyPercent': 'float64'})
```

In theory, you can have Dask sample more records by specifying more bytes with the `sample` parameter, but this does not currently fix the problem. The current sampling code does not strictly respect the number of bytes requested.

Even when schema inference does not return an error, depending on it has a number of drawbacks. Schema inference involves sampling data, and its results are therefore both probabilistic and slow. When you can, you should use self-describing formats or otherwise avoid schema inference; your data loading will be faster and more reliable. Some common self-describing formats you may encounter include Parquet, Avro, and ORC.

Reading and writing from/to new file formats is a lot of work, especially if there are no existing Python libraries. If there are existing libraries, you might find it easier to read the raw data into a bag and parse it with a `map` function, which we will explore further in the next chapter.

Dask does not detect sorted data on load. Instead, if you have presorted data, add the `sorted=true` parameter when setting an index to take advantage of your already sorted data, a step you will learn about in the next section. If you specify this when the data is not sorted, however, you may get silent data corruption.

You can also connect Dask to databases or microservices. Relational databases are a fantastic tool and are often quite performant at both simple reads and writes. Often relational databases support distributed deployment whereby the data is split up on multiple nodes, and this is mostly used with large datasets. Relational databases tend to be great at handling transactions at scale, but running analytic capabilities on the same node can encounter issues. Dask can be used to efficiently read and compute over SQL databases.

You can use Dask's built-in support for loading SQL databases using SQLAlchemy. For Dask to split up the query on multiple machines, you need to give it an index key. Often SQL databases will have a primary key or numerical index key that you can use for this purpose (e.g., read_sql_table("customers", index_col="customer_id")). An example of this is shown in Example 4-4.

Example 4-4. Reading from and writing to SQL with Dask DataFrame

```
from sqlite3 import connect
from sqlalchemy import sql
import dask.dataframe as dd

#sqlite connection
db_conn = "sqlite://fake_school.sql"
db = connect(db_conn)

col_student_num = sql.column("student_number")
col_grade = sql.column("grade")
tbl_transcript = sql.table("transcripts")

select_statement = sql.select([col_student_num,
                               col_grade]
                             ).select_from(tbl_transcript)

#read from sql db
ddf = dd.read_sql_query(select_stmt,
                        npartitions=4,
                        index_col=col_student_num,
                        con=db_conn)

#alternatively, read whole table
ddf = dd.read_sql_table("transcripts",
                        db_conn,
                        index_col="student_number",
                        npartitions=4
                        )

#do_some_ETL...

#save to db
ddf.to_sql("transcript_analytics",
```

```
    uri=db_conn,
    if_exists='replace',
    schema=None,
    index=False
    )
```

More advanced connections to databases or microservices are best made using the bag interface and writing your custom load code, which you will learn more about in the next chapter.

Partitioned Reads and Writes with Parquet

The least expensive data to process is the data you never have to read. If you need only a subset of the files (or columns), limiting your reads can greatly speed up your processing. Similarly, when writing your data out, if downstream users are likely going to need only subsets of the data, it can be helpful to write data so consumers can read only the files or columns they need.

 Dask implements only filtered reads and writes for Parquet. If you are reading data in another partitioned format, you can ignore the filtering or manually compute the required files. There is no easy way to implement partitioned writes for other formats.

Parquet is a self-describing format, which means it holds the schema/type information. The data is stored in a columnar format that allows for reading just the columns you care about. If you need only some of the columns, pass the columns= flag when calling read_parquet.

If you are loading data from Parquet with partitioning on the key that you care about, you should add the filter to the read_parquet. This filter is not an arbitrary expression; rather, it is a tuple of key, operation, value. The key is a string representing the column. The operation is a string and one of ==, <, <=, >, >=, !=, in, or not in. The value is either a single value or a list of values you are interested in loading.

While Dask has limited support for query push-down with partition reads, many other tools can automatically reduce the data read if it follows a known partitioning function. When you write data out, you can have Dask write the data to different directories based on partitioning keys by adding partition_on.

On the flip side, if most of your downstream users consume all of the table or have unique columns they are filtering on, a partitioned write can decrease performance. Since listing files on a network filesystem is not free, discovering the files becomes more expensive when you have partitioned writes that you are not taking advantage of.

Other systems commonly use metastores for partitioned reads and writes when dealing with large data sizes. Dask does not presently have the built-in ability to talk to a metastore such as Iceberg, Hive, or Delta Lake. Metastores can be useful for loading subset tables and time-traveling (looking at old versions) when needed. The Dask deltatable library (*https://oreil.ly/2i2Dd*) integrates reading the Delta Lake table. Iceberg has a built-in Python API (*https://oreil.ly/tIP9S*) that you can use to get a list of files associated with a particular query and then use Dask's existing file APIs on top of it. We expect the integrations with metastores will continue to improve rapidly.

Filesystems

Loading data can be a substantial amount of work and a bottleneck, so Dask distributes this like most other tasks. If you are using Dask distributed, each worker must have access to the files to parallelize the loading. Rather than copying the file to each worker, network filesystems allow everyone to access the files. Dask's file access layer uses the FSSPEC library (from the intake project) to access the different filesystems. Since FSSPEC supports a range of filesystems, it does not install the requirements for every supported filesystem. Use the code in Example 4-5 to see which filesystems are supported and which ones need additional packages.

Example 4-5. Getting a list of FSSPEC-supported filesystems

```
from fsspec.registry import known_implementations
known_implementations
```

Many filesystems require some kind of configuration, be it endpoint or credentials. Often new filesystems, like MinIO, offer S3-compatible APIs but overload the endpoint and require some extra configuration to function. With Dask you specify the configuration parameters to the read/write function with `storage_options`. Everyone's configuration here will likely be a bit different.[2] Dask will use your `storage_options` dict as the keyword arguments to the underlying FSSPEC implementation. For example, my `storage_options` for MinIO are shown in Example 4-6.

Example 4-6. Configuring Dask to talk to MinIO

```
minio_storage_options = {
    "key": "YOURACCESSKEY",
    "secret": "YOURSECRETKEY",
    "client_kwargs": {
        "endpoint_url": "http://minio-1602984784.minio.svc.cluster.local:9000",
        "region_name": 'us-east-1'
```

---

2 FSSPEC documentation (*https://oreil.ly/ZfcRv*) includes the specifics for configuring each of the backends.

```
    },
    "config_kwargs": {"s3": {"signature_version": 's3v4'}},
}
```

> ### Compression
>
> Compression reduces storage costs, making it popular, and the same library used
> to abstract filesystem access in Dask also abstracts compression. Some compression
> algorithms support random reads, but many do not. For people coming from the
> Hadoop ecosystem, this can be thought of as the impact on "splittable."
>
> Dask's reading and writing functions take the parameter `compression` to specify the
> compression algorithm used. One of the most popular options is `gzip`.
>
> Just because the underlying compression algorithm may support random reads does
> not mean that the FSSPEC wrapper will. Unfortunately, there is no current, easy way
> to check what a compression format supports besides testing it out or reading the
> source code.
>
> Dask does not support "streaming" non-random access input formats. This means
> that the data inside each file must fit entirely in memory.

Indexing

Indexing into a DataFrame is one of the powerful features of pandas, but it comes
with some restrictions when moving into a distributed system like Dask. Since Dask
does not track the size of each partition, positional indexing by row is not supported.
You can use positional indexing for columns, as well as label indexing for columns or
rows.

Indexing is frequently used to filter the data to have only the components you need.
We did this for the San Francisco COVID-19 data by looking at just the case rates for
people of all vaccine statuses, as shown in Example 4-7.

Example 4-7. Dask DataFrame indexing

```
mini_sf_covid_df = (sf_covid_df
                    [sf_covid_df['vaccination_status'] == 'All']
                    [['specimen_collection_date', 'new_cases']])
```

If you truly need positional indexing by row, you can implement your own by
computing the size of each partition and using this to select the desired partition
subsets. This is very inefficient, so Dask avoids implementing it directly; make an
intentional choice before doing this.

Shuffles

As mentioned in the previous chapter, shuffles are expensive. The primary causes of the expensive nature of shuffles are the serialization overhead in moving data between processes and the comparative slowness of networks relative to reading data from memory. These costs scale as the amount of data being shuffled increases, so Dask has techniques to reduce the amount of data being shuffled. These techniques depend on certain data properties or the operation being performed.

Rolling Windows and map_overlap

One situation that can trigger the need for a shuffle is a rolling window, where at the edges of a partition your function needs some records from its neighbors. Dask DataFrame has a special map_overlap function in which you can specify a *look-after* window (also called a *look-ahead* window) and *look-behind* window (also called a *look-back* window) of rows to transfer (either an integer or a time delta). The simplest example taking advantage of this is a rolling average, shown in Example 4-8.

Example 4-8. Dask DataFrame rolling average

```
def process_overlap_window(df):
    return df.rolling('5D').mean()


rolling_avg = partitioned_df.map_overlap(
    process_overlap_window,
    pd.Timedelta('5D'),
    0)
```

Using map_overlap allows Dask to transfer only the data needed. For this implementation to work correctly, your minimum partition size needs to be larger than your largest window.

 Dask's rolling windows will not cross multiple partitions. If your DataFrame is partitioned so that the look-after or look-back is greater than the length of the neighbor's partition, the results will either fail or be incorrect. Dask validates this for time delta look-after, but no such checks are performed for look-backs or integer look-after.

An effective but expensive technique for working around the single-partition look-ahead/look-behind of Dask is to repartition your Dask DataFrames.

Aggregations

Aggregations are another special case that can reduce the amount of data that needs to be transferred over the network. Aggregations are functions that combine records. If you are coming from a map/reduce or Spark background, reduceByKey is the classic aggregation. Aggregations can either be "by key" or be global across an entire DataFrame.

To aggregate by key, you first need to call groupby with the column(s) representing the key, or the keying function to aggregate on. For example, calling df.groupby("PostCode") groups your DataFrame by postal code, or calling df.groupby(["PostCode", "SicCodes"]) uses a combination of columns for grouping. Function-wise, many of the same pandas aggregates are available, but the performance of aggregates in Dask are very different from local pandas DataFrames.

 If you're aggregating by partition key, Dask can compute the aggregation without needing a shuffle.

The first way to speed up your aggregations is to reduce the columns that you are aggregating on, since the fastest data to process is no data. Finally, when possible, doing multiple aggregations at the same time reduces the number of times the same data needs to be shuffled. Therefore, if you need to compute the average and the max, you should compute both at the same time (see Example 4-9).

Example 4-9. Dask DataFrame max and mean

```
dask.compute(
    raw_grouped[["new_cases"]].max(),
    raw_grouped[["new_cases"]].mean())
```

For distributed systems like Dask, if an aggregation can be partially evaluated and then merged, you can potentially combine some records pre-shuffle. Not all partial aggregations are created equal. What matters with partial aggregations is that the amount of data is reduced when merging values with the same key compared to the original multiple values.

The most efficient aggregations take a sublinear amount of space regardless of the number of records. Some of these, such as sum, count, first, minimum, maximum, mean, and standard deviation, can take constant space. More complicated tasks, like quantiles and distinct counts, also have sublinear approximation options. These approximation options can be great, as exact answers can require linear growth in storage.[3]

Some aggregation functions are not sublinear in growth, but tend to or might not grow too quickly. Counting the distinct values is in this group, but if all your values are unique there is no space saving.

To take advantage of efficient aggregations, you need to use a built-in aggregation from Dask, or write your own using Dask's aggregation class. Whenever you can, use a built-in. Built-ins not only require less effort but also are often faster. Not all of the pandas aggregates are directly supported in Dask, so sometimes your only choice is to write your own aggregate.

If you choose to write your own aggregate, you have three functions to define: chunk for handling each group-partition/chunk, agg to combine the results of chunk between partitions, and (optionally) finalize to take the result of agg and produce a final value.

The fastest way to understand how to use partial aggregation is by looking at an example that uses all three functions. Using the weighted average in Example 4-10 can help you think of what is needed for each function. The first function needs to compute the weighted values and the weights. The agg function combines these by summing each side part of the tuple. Finally, the finalize function divides the total by the weights.

Example 4-10. Dask custom aggregate

```python
# Write a custom weighted mean, we get either a DataFrameGroupBy
# with multiple columns or SeriesGroupBy for each chunk
def process_chunk(chunk):
    def weighted_func(df):
        return (df["EmployerSize"] * df["DiffMeanHourlyPercent"]).sum()
    return (chunk.apply(weighted_func), chunk.sum()["EmployerSize"])


def agg(total, weights):
    return (total.sum(), weights.sum())


def finalize(total, weights):
    return total / weights
```

---

3 This can lead to out-of-memory exceptions while executing the aggregation. The linear growth in storage requires that (within a constant factor) all the data must be able to fit on a single process, which limits how effective Dask can be.

```
weighted_mean = dd.Aggregation(
    name='weighted_mean',
    chunk=process_chunk,
    agg=agg,
    finalize=finalize)

aggregated = (df_diff_with_emp_size.groupby("PostCode")
                 ["EmployerSize", "DiffMeanHourlyPercent"].agg(weighted_mean))
```

In some cases, such as with a pure summation, you don't need to do any post-processing on agg's output, so you can skip the finalize function.

Not all aggregations must be by key; you can also compute aggregations across all rows. Dask's custom aggregation interface, however, is exposed only with by-key operations.

Dask's built-in full DataFrame aggregations use a lower-level interface called apply_contact_apply for partial aggregations. Rather than learn two different APIs for partial aggregations, we prefer to do a static groupby by providing a constant grouping function. This way, we only have to know one interface for aggregations. You can use this to find the aggregate COVID-19 numbers across the DataFrame, as shown in Example 4-11.

Example 4-11. Aggregating across the entire DataFrame

```
raw_grouped = sf_covid_df.groupby(lambda x: 0)
```

When built-in aggregation exists, it will likely be better than anything we would write. Sometimes a partial aggregation is partially implemented, as in the case of Dask's HyperLogLog: it is implemented only for full DataFrames. You can often translate simple aggregations using apply_contact_apply or aca by copying the chunk function, using the combine parameter for agg, and using the aggregate parameter for finalize. This is shown via porting Dask's HyperLogLog implementation in Example 4-12.

Example 4-12. Wrapping Dask's HyperLogLog in dd.Aggregation

```
# Wrap Dask's hyperloglog in dd.Aggregation

from dask.dataframe import hyperloglog

approx_unique = dd.Aggregation(
    name='approx_unique',
    chunk=hyperloglog.compute_hll_array,
    agg=hyperloglog.reduce_state,
    finalize=hyperloglog.estimate_count)
```

```
aggregated = (df_diff_with_emp_size.groupby("PostCode")
              ["EmployerSize", "DiffMeanHourlyPercent"].agg(weighted_mean))
```

Slow/inefficient aggregations (or those very likely to cause an out-of-memory exception) use storage proportional to the records being aggregated. Examples from this slow group include making a list and naively computing exact quantiles.[4] With these slow aggregates, using Dask's aggregation class has no benefit over the `apply` API, which you may wish to use for simplicity. For example, if you just wanted a list of employer IDs by postal code, rather than having to write three functions you could use a one-liner like `df.groupby("PostCode")["EmployerId"].apply(lambda g: list(g))`. Dask implements the `apply` function as a full shuffle, which is covered in the next section.

 Dask is unable to apply partial aggregations when you use the `apply` function.

Full Shuffles and Partitioning

If an operation seems to be slower inside of Dask than you would expect from working in local DataFrames, it might be because it requires a full shuffle. An example of this is sorting, which is inherently expensive in distributed systems because it most often requires a shuffle. Full shuffles are sometimes an unavoidable part of working in Dask. Counterintuitively, while full shuffles are themselves slow, you can use them to speed up future operations that are all happening on the same grouping key(s). As mentioned in the aggregation section, one of the ways a full shuffle is triggered is by using the `apply` method when partitioning is not aligned.

Partitioning

You will most commonly use full shuffles to repartition your data. It's important to have the right partitioning when dealing with aggregations, rolling windows, or look-ups/indexing. As discussed in the rolling window section, Dask cannot do more than one partition's worth of look-ahead or look-behind, so having the right partitioning is required to get the correct results. For most other operations, having incorrect partitioning will slow down your job.

Dask has three primary methods for controlling the partitioning of a DataFrame: `set_index`, `repartition`, and `shuffle` (see Table 4-1). You use `set_index` when changing the partitioning to a new key/index. `repartition` keeps the same key/index

---

4 Alternate algorithms for exact quantiles depend on more shuffles to reduce the space overhead.

but changes the splits. `repartition` and `set_index` take similar parameters, with `repartition` not taking an index key name. In general, if you are not changing the column used for the index, you should use `repartition`. `shuffle` is a bit different since it does not produce a known partitioning scheme that operations like `groupby` can take advantage of.

Table 4-1. Functions to control partitioning

Method	Changes index key	Sets number of partitions	Results in a known partitioning scheme	Ideal use case
`set_index`	Yes	Yes	Yes	Changing the index key
`repartition`	No	Yes	Yes	Increasing/decreasing number of partitions
`shuffle`	No	Yes	No	Skewed distribution of key[a]

[a] Hashes the key for distribution, which can help randomly distribute skewed data *if* the keys are unique (but clustered).

The first step in getting the right partitioning for your DataFrame is to decide whether you want an index. Indexes are useful when filtering data by an indexed value, indexing, grouping, and for almost any other by-key operation. One such by-key operation would be a `groupby`, in which the column being grouped on could be a good candidate for the key. If you use a rolling window over a column, that column must be the key, which makes choosing the key relatively easy. Once you've decided on an index, you can call `set_index` with the column name of the index (e.g., `set_index("PostCode")`). This will, under most circumstances, result in a shuffle, so it's a good time to size your partitions.

> If you're unsure what the current key used for partitioning is, you can check the `index` property to see the partitioning key.

Once you've chosen your key, the next question is how to size your partitions. The advice in "Partitioning/Chunking Collections" on page 24 generally applies here: shoot for enough partitions to keep each machine busy, but keep in mind the general sweet spot of 100 MB to 1 GB. Dask generally computes pretty even splits if you give it a target number of partitions.[5] Thankfully, `set_index` will also take `npartitions`. To repartition the data by postal code, with 10 partitions, you would add `set_index("PostCode", npartitions=10)`; otherwise Dask will default to the number of input partitions.

---

5 Key-skew can make this impossible for a known partitioner.

If you plan to use rolling windows, you will likely need to ensure that you have the right size (in terms of key range) covered in each partition. To do this as part of set_index, you would need to compute your own divisions to ensure each partition has the right range of records present. Divisions are specified as a list starting from the minimal value of the first partition up to the maximum value of the last partition. Each value in between is a "cut" point between the pandas DataFrames that make up the Dask DataFrame. To make a DataFrame with partitions [0, 100) [100, 200), [200, 300), [300, 500), you would write df.set_index("NumEmployees", divisions=[0, 100, 200, 300, 500]). Similarly, for the date range to support a rolling window of up to seven days from around the start of the COVID-19 pandemic to today, see Example 4-13.

Example 4-13. Dask DataFrame rolling window with set_index

```
divisions = pd.date_range(
    start="2021-01-01",
    end=datetime.today(),
    freq='7D').tolist()
partitioned_df_as_part_of_set_index = mini_sf_covid_df.set_index(
    'specimen_collection_date', divisions=divisions)
```

Dask, including for rolling time windows, assumes that your partition index is monotonically increasing.[6]

So far, you've had to specify the number of partitions, or the specific divisions, but you might be wondering if Dask can just figure that out itself. Thankfully, Dask's repartition function has the ability to pick divisions for a given target size, as shown in Example 4-14. However, doing this has a non-trivial cost, as Dask must evaluate the DataFrame as well as the repartition itself.

Example 4-14. Dask DataFrame automatic partitioning

```
reparted = indexed.repartition(partition_size="20kb")
```

Dask's set_index has a similar partition_size parameter but, as of this writing, works only to reduce the number of partitions (*https://oreil.ly/3I9Gm*).

---

6 Strictly increasing with no repeated values (e.g., 1, 4, 7 is monotonically increasing, but 1, 4, 4, 7 is not).

As you saw at the start of this chapter, when writing a DataFrame, each partition is given its own file, but sometimes this can result in files that are too big or too small. Some tools can accept only one file as input, so you need to repartition everything into a single partition. At other times, the data storage system is optimized for a certain file size, like the HDFS default block size of 128 MB. The good news is that techniques such as repartition and set_index solve these problems for you.

Embarrassingly Parallel Operations

Dask's map_partitions function applies a function to each of the partitions underlying pandas DataFrames, and the result is also a pandas DataFrame. Functions implemented with map_partitions are embarrassingly parallel since they don't require any inter-worker transfer of data.[7] Dask implements map with map_partitions, as well as many row-wise operations. If you want to use a row-wise operation that you find missing, you can implement it yourself, as shown in Example 4-15.

Example 4-15. Dask DataFrame fillna

```
def fillna(df):
    return df.fillna(value={"PostCode": "UNKNOWN"}).fillna(value=0)


new_df = df.map_partitions(fillna)
# Since there could be an NA in the index clear the partition / division
# information
new_df.clear_divisions()
```

You aren't limited to calling pandas built-ins. Provided that your function takes and returns a DataFrame, you can do pretty much anything you want inside map _partitions.

The full pandas API is too long to cover in this chapter, but if a function can operate on a row-by-row basis without any knowledge of the rows before or after, it may already be implemented in Dask DataFrames using map_partitions.

When using map_partitions on a DataFrame, you can change anything about each row, including the key that it is partitioned on. If you *are* changing the values in the partition key, you *must* either clear the partitioning information on the resulting DataFrame with clear_divisions() *or* specify the correct indexing with set_index, which you'll learn more about in the next section.

---

7 Embarrassingly parallel problems (*https://oreil.ly/30938*) are ones in which the overhead of distributed computing and communication is low.

Incorrect partitioning information can result in incorrect results, not just exceptions, as Dask may miss relevant data.

Working with Multiple DataFrames

Pandas and Dask have four common functions for combining DataFrames. At the root is the `concat` function, which allows you to join DataFrames on any axis. Concatenating DataFrames is generally slower in Dask since it involves inter-worker communication. The other three functions are `join`, `merge`, and `append`, all of which implement special cases for common situations on top of `concat` and have slightly different performance considerations. Having good divisions/partitioning, in terms of key selection and number of partitions, makes a huge difference when working on multiple DataFrames.

Dask's `join` and `merge` functions take most of the standard pandas arguments along with an extra optional one, `npartitions`. `npartitions` specifies a target number of output partitions, but it is used only for hash joins (which you'll learn about in "Multi-DataFrame Internals" on page 52). Both functions automatically repartition your input DataFrames if needed. This is great, as you might not know the partitioning, but since repartitioning can be slow, explicitly using the lower-level `concat` function when you don't expect any partitioning changes to be needed can help catch performance problems early. Dask's `join` can take more than two DataFrames at a time only when doing a *left* or *outer* join type.

Dask has special logic to speed up multi-DataFrame joins, so in most cases, rather than doing `a.join(b).join(c).join(d).join(e)`, you will benefit from doing `a.join([b, c, d, e])`. However, if you are performing a left join with a small dataset, then the first syntax may be more efficient.

When you combine or `concat` DataFrames by row (similar to a SQL UNION), the performance depends on whether divisions of the DataFrames being combined are *well ordered*. We call the divisions of a series of DataFrames well ordered if all the divisions are known and the highest division of the previous DataFrame is below that of the lowest division of the next. If any input has an unknown division, Dask will produce an output without known partitioning. With all known partitions, Dask treats row-based concatenations as a metadata-only change and will not perform any shuffle. This requires that there is no overlap between the divisions. There is also an extra `interleave_partitions` parameter, which will change the join type for row-based combinations to one without the input partitioning restriction and result in a known partitioner. Dask DataFrames with known partitioners can support faster look-ups and operations by key.

Dask's column-based `concat` (similar to a SQL JOIN) also has restrictions around the divisions/partitions of the DataFrames it is combining. Dask's version of `concat` supports only inner or full outer join, not left or right. Column-based joins require that all inputs have known partitioners and also result in a DataFrame with known partitioning. Having a known partitioner can be useful for subsequent joins.

 Don't use Dask's `concat` when operating by row on a DataFrame with unknown divisions, as it will likely return incorrect results.[8]

Multi-DataFrame Internals

Dask uses four techniques—hash, broadcast, partitioned, and `stack_partitions`—to combine DataFrames, and each has very different performance. These four functions do not map 1:1 with the join functions you choose from. Rather, Dask chooses the technique based on the indexes, divisions, and requested join type (e.g., outer/left/inner). The three column-based join techniques are hash joins, broadcast joins, and partitioned joins. When doing row-based combinations (e.g., `append`), Dask has a special technique called `stack_partitions` that is extra fast. It's important that you understand the performance of each of these techniques and the conditions that will cause Dask to pick each approach:

Hash joins
   The default that Dask uses when no other join technique is suitable. Hash joins shuffle the data for all the input DataFrames to partition on the target key. They use the hash values of keys, which results in a DataFrame that is not in any particular order. As such, the result of a hash join does not have any known divisions.

Broadcast joins
   Ideal for joining large DataFrames with small DataFrames. In a broadcast join, Dask takes the smaller DataFrame and distributes it to all the workers. This means that the smaller DataFrame must be able to fit in memory. To tell Dask that a DataFrame is a good candidate for broadcasting, you make sure it is all stored in one partition, such as by calling `repartition(npartitions=1)`.

---

8 Dask assumes the indices are aligned when there are no indices present.

Partitioned joins

Occur when combining DataFrames along an index where the partitions/divisions are known for all the DataFrames. Since the input partitions are known, Dask is able to align the partitions between the DataFrames, involving less data transfer, as each output partition has less than a full set of inputs.

Since partitioned and broadcast joins are faster, doing some work to help Dask can be worth it. For example, concatenating several DataFrames with known and aligned partitions/divisions and one unaligned DataFrame will result in an expensive hash join. Instead, try to either set the index and partition on the remaining DataFrame or join the less expensive DataFrames first and then perform the expensive join after.

The fourth technique, `stack_partitions`, is different from the other options since it doesn't involve any movement of data. Instead, the resulting DataFrame partitions list is a union of the upstream partitions from the input DataFrames. Dask uses `stack_partitions` for most row-based combinations except when all of the input DataFrame divisions are known, they are not well ordered, and you ask Dask to `interleave_partitions`. The `stack_partitions` technique is able to provide known partitioning in its output only when the input divisions are known and well ordered. If all of the divisions are known but not well ordered and you set `interleave _partitions`, Dask will use a partitioned join instead. While this approach is comparatively inexpensive, it is not free, and it can result in an excessively large number of partitions, requiring you to repartition anyway.

Missing Functionality

Not all multi-DataFrame operations are implemented, like `compare`, which leads us into the next section about the limitations of Dask DataFrames.

What Does Not Work

Dask's DataFrame implements most, but not all, of the pandas DataFrame API. Some of the pandas API is not implemented in Dask because of the development time involved. Other parts are not used to avoid exposing an API that would be unexpectedly slow.

Sometimes the API is just missing small parts, as both pandas and Dask are under active development. An example is the `split` function from Example 2-10. In local pandas, instead of doing `split().explode()`, you could have called `split(expand=true)`. Some of these missing parts can be excellent places for you to get involved and contribute to the Dask project (*https://oreil.ly/Txd_R*) if you are interested.

Some libraries do not parallelize as well as others. In these cases, a common approach is to try to filter or aggregate the data down enough that it can be represented locally and then apply the local libraries to the data. For example, with graphing, it's common to pre-aggregate the counts or take a random sample and graph the result.

While much of the pandas DataFrame API will work, before you swap in Dask DataFrame, it's important to make sure you have good test coverage to catch the situations where it does not.

What's Slower

Usually, using Dask DataFrames will improve performance, but not always. Generally, smaller datasets will perform better in local pandas. As discussed, anything involving shuffles is generally slower in a distributed system than in a local one. Iterative algorithms can also produce large graphs of operations, which are slow to evaluate in Dask compared to traditional greedy evaluation.

Some problems are generally unsuitable for data-parallel computing. For example, writing out to a data store with a single lock that has more parallel writers will increase the lock contention and may make it slower than if a single thread was doing the writing. In these situations, you can sometimes repartition your data or write individual partitions to avoid lock contention.

Handling Recursive Algorithms

Dask's lazy evaluation, powered by its lineage graph, is normally beneficial, allowing it to combine steps automatically. However, when the graph gets too large, Dask can struggle to manage it, which often shows up as a slow driver process or notebook, and sometimes as an out-of-memory exception. Thankfully, you can work around this by writing out your DataFrame and reading it back in. Generally, Parquet is the best format for doing this as it is space-efficient and self-describing, so no schema inference is required.

Re-computed Data

Another challenge of lazy evaluation is if you want to reuse an element multiple times. For example, say you want to load a few DataFrames and then compute multiple pieces of information. You can ask Dask to keep a collection (including DataFrame, series, etc.) in memory by running `client.persist(collection)`. Not all re-computed data needs to be avoided; for example, if loading the DataFrames is fast enough, it might be fine not to persist them.

Like other functions in Dask, `persist()` does not modify the Data-Frame—and if you call functions on it you will still have your data re-computed. This is notably different from Apache Spark.

How Other Functions Are Different

For performance reasons, various parts of Dask DataFrames behave a little differently than local DataFrames:

reset_index
>   The index will start back over at zero on each partition.

kurtosis
>   This function does not filter out NaNs and uses SciPy defaults.

concat
>   Instead of coercing category types, each category type is expanded to the union of all the categories it is concatenated with.

sort_values
>   Dask supports only single-column sorts.

Joining multiple DataFrames
>   When joining more than two DataFrames at the same time, the join type must be either outer or left.

When porting your code to use Dask DataFrames, you should be especially mindful anytime you use these functions, as they might not exactly work in the axis you intended. Work small first and test the correctness of the numbers, as issues can often be tricky to track down.

When porting existing pandas code to Dask, consider using the local single-machine version to produce test datasets to compare the results with, to ensure that all changes are intentional.

Data Science with Dask DataFrame: Putting It Together

Dask DataFrame has already proven to be a popular framework for big data uses, so we wanted to highlight a common use case and considerations. Here, we use a canonical data science challenge dataset, the New York City yellow taxicab, and walk through what a data engineer working with this dataset might consider. In the subsequent chapters covering ML workloads, we will be using many of the DataFrame tools to build on.

Deciding to Use Dask

As discussed earlier, Dask excels in data-parallel tasks. A particularly good fit is a dataset that may already be available in columnar format, like Parquet. We also assess where the data lives, such as in S3 or in other remote storage options. Many data scientists and engineers would probably have a dataset that cannot be contained on a single machine or cannot be stored locally due to compliance constraints. Dask's design lends itself well to these use cases.

Our NYC taxi data fits all these criteria: the data is stored in S3 by the City of New York in Parquet format, and it is easily scalable up and down, as it is partitioned by dates. Additionally, we evaluate that the data is structured already, so we can use Dask DataFrame. Since Dask DataFrames and pandas DataFrames are similar, we can also use a lot of existing workflows for pandas. We can sample a few of these, do our exploratory data analysis in a smaller dev environment, and then scale it up to the full dataset, all with the same code. Note that for Example 4-16, we use row groups to specify chunking behavior.

Example 4-16. Dask DataFrame loading multiple Parquet files

```
filename = './nyc_taxi/*.parquet'
df_x = dd.read_parquet(
    filename,
    split_row_groups=2
)
```

Exploratory Data Analysis with Dask

The first step of data science often consists of exploratory data analysis (EDA), or understanding the dataset and plotting its shape. Here, we use Dask DataFrames to walk through the process and examine the common troubleshooting issues that arise from nuanced differences between pandas DataFrame and Dask DataFrame.

Loading Data

The first time you load the data into your dev environment, you might encounter block size issues or schema issues. While Dask tries to infer both, at times it cannot. Block size issues will often show up when you call `.compute()` on trivial code and see one worker hitting the memory ceiling. In that case, some manual work would be involved in determining the right chunk size. Schema issues would show up as an error or a warning as you read the data, or in subtle ways later on, such as mismatching float32 and float64. If you know the schema already, it's a good idea to enforce that by specifying dtypes at reading.

As you further explore a dataset, you might encounter data printed by default in a format that you don't like, for example, scientific notation. The control for that is through pandas, not Dask itself. Dask implicitly calls pandas, so you want to explicitly set your preferred format using pandas.

Summary statistics on the data work just like `.describe()` from pandas, along with specified percentiles or `.quantile()`. Remember to chain multiple computes together if you are running several of these, which will save compute time back and forth. Using Dask DataFrame `describe` is shown in Example 4-17.

Example 4-17. Dask DataFrame describing percentiles with pretty formatting

```
import pandas as pd

pd.set_option('display.float_format', lambda x: '%.5f' % x)
df.describe(percentiles=[.25, .5, .75]).compute()
```

Plotting Data

Plotting data is often an important step in getting to know your dataset. Plotting big data is a tricky subject. We as data engineers often get around that issue by first working with a smaller sampled dataset. For that, Dask would work alongside a Python plotting library such as matplotlib or seaborn, just like pandas. The advantage of Dask DataFrame is that we are now able to plot the entire dataset, if desired. We can use plotting frameworks along with Dask to plot the entire dataset. Here, Dask does the filtering, the aggregation on the distributed workers, and then collects down to one worker to give to a non-distributed library like matplotlib to render. Plotting a Dask DataFrame is shown in Example 4-18.

Example 4-18. Dask DataFrame plotting trip distance

```
import matplotlib.pyplot as plt
import seaborn as sns
import numpy as np

get_ipython().run_line_magic('matplotlib', 'inline')
sns.set(style="white", palette="muted", color_codes=True)
f, axes = plt.subplots(1, 1, figsize=(11, 7), sharex=True)
sns.despine(left=True)
sns.distplot(
    np.log(
        df['trip_distance'].values +
        1),
    axlabel='Log(trip_distance)',
    label='log(trip_distance)',
    bins=50,
    color="r")
```

```
plt.setp(axes, yticks=[])
plt.tight_layout()
plt.show()
```

Note that if you're used to the NumPy logic, you will have to think of the Dask DataFrame layer when plotting. For example, NumPy users would be familiar with df[col].values syntax for defining plotting variables. The .values mean a different action in Dask; what we pass is df[col] instead.

Inspecting Data

Pandas DataFrame users would be familiar with .loc() and .iloc() for inspecting data at a particular row or column. This logic translates to Dask DataFrame, with important differences in .iloc() behaviors.

A sufficiently large Dask DataFrame will contain multiple pandas DataFrames. This changes the way we should think about numbering and addressing indices. For example, .iloc() (a way to access the positions by index) doesn't work exactly the same for Dask, since each smaller DataFrame would have its own .iloc() value, and Dask does not track the size of each smaller DataFrame. In other words, a global index value is hard for Dask to figure out, since Dask will have to iteratively count through each DataFrame to get to an index. Users should check .iloc() on their DataFrame and ensure that indices return the correct values.

Be aware that calling methods like .reset_index() can reset indices in each of the smaller DataFrames, potentially returning multiple values when users call .iloc().

Conclusion

In this chapter, you've learned how to understand what kinds of operations are slower than you might expect with Dask. You've also gained a number of techniques to deal with the performance differences between pandas DataFrames and Dask DataFrames. By understanding the situations in which Dask DataFrames performance may not meet your needs, you've also gained an understanding of what problems are not well suited to Dask. So that you can put this all together, you've also learned about Dask DataFrame IO options. From here you will go on to learn more about Dask's other collections and then how to move beyond collections.

In this chapter, you have learned what may cause your Dask DataFrames to behave differently or more slowly than you might expect. This same understanding of how Dask DataFrames are implemented can help you decide whether distributed Data-Frames are well suited to your problem. You've also seen how to get datasets larger than a single machine can handle into and out of Dask's DataFrames.

## CHAPTER 5

Dask's Collections

So far you've seen the basics of how Dask is built as well as how Dask uses these building blocks to support data science with DataFrames. This chapter explores where Dask's bag and array interfaces—often overlooked, relative to DataFrames—are more appropriate. As mentioned in "Hello Worlds" on page 10, Dask bags implement common functional APIs, and Dask arrays implement a subset of NumPy arrays.

 Understanding partitioning is important for understanding collections. If you skipped "Partitioning/Chunking Collections" on page 24, now is a good time to head back and take a look.

Dask Arrays

Dask arrays implement a subset of the NumPy ndarray interface, making them ideal for porting code that uses NumPy to run on Dask. Much of your understanding from the previous chapter with DataFrames carries over to Dask arrays, as well as much of your understanding of ndarrays.

Common Use Cases

Some common use cases for Dask arrays include:

- Large-scale imaging and astronomy data
- Weather data
- Multi-dimensional data

Similar to Dask DataFrames and pandas, if you wouldn't use an nparray for the problem at a smaller scale, a Dask array may not be the right solution.

When Not to Use Dask Arrays

If your data fits in memory on a single computer, using Dask arrays is unlikely to give you many benefits over nparrays, especially compared to local accelerators like Numba. Numba is well suited to vectorizing and parallelizing local tasks with and without Graphics Processing Units (GPUs). You can use Numba with or without Dask, and we'll look at how to further speed up Dask arrays using Numba in Chapter 10.

Dask arrays, like their local counterpart, require that data is all of the same type. This means that they cannot be used for semi-structured or mixed-type data (think strings and ints).

Loading/Saving

As with Dask DataFrames, loading and writing functions start with to_ or read_ as the prefixes. Each format has its own configuration, but in general, the first positional argument is the location of the data to be read. The location can be a wildcard path of files (e.g., *s3://test-bucket/magic/**), a list of files, or a regular file location.

Dask arrays support reading the following formats:

- zarr
- npy stacks (only local disk)

And reading from and writing to:

- hdf5
- zarr
- tiledb
- npy stacks (local disk only)

In addition, you can convert Dask arrays to/from Dask bags and DataFrames (provided the types are compatible). As you may have noted, Dask does not support reading arrays from as many formats as you might expect, which provides the opportunity for an excellent use of bags (covered in the next section).

What's Missing

While Dask arrays implement a large amount of the ndarray APIs, it is not a complete set. As with Dask DataFrames, some of the omissions are intentional (e.g., sort,

---

much of linalg, etc., which would be slow), and other parts are just missing because no one has had the time to implement them yet.

Special Dask Functions

Since, as with distributed DataFrames, the partitioned nature of Dask arrays makes performance a bit different, there are some unique Dask array functions not found in numpy.linalg:

map_overlap
> You can use this for any windowed view of the data, as with map_overlap on Dask DataFrames.

map_blocks
> This is similar to Dask's DataFrames map_partitions, and you can use it for implementing embarrassingly parallel operations that the standard Dask library has not yet implemented, including new element-wise functions in NumPy.

topk
> This returns the topk elements of the array in place of fully sorting it (which is much more expensive).[1]

compute_chunk_sizes
> Dask needs to know the chunk sizes to support indexing; if an array has unknown chunk sizes, you can call this function.

These special functions are not present on the underlying regular collections, as they do not offer the same performance savings in non-parallel/non-distributed environments.

Dask Bags

To continue to draw parallels to Python's internal data structures, you can think of bags as slightly different lists or sets. Bags are like lists except without the concept of order (so there are no indexing operations). Alternatively, if you think of bags like sets, the difference between them is that bags allow duplicates. Dask's bags have the least number of restrictions on what they contain and similarly have the smallest API. In fact, Examples 2-6 through 2-9 covered most of the core of the APIs for bags.

---

1 topk (*https://oreil.ly/vUjgv*) extracts the topk elements of each partition and then only needs to shuffle the k elements out of each partition.

For users coming from Apache Spark, Dask bags are most closely related to Spark's RDDs.

Common Use Cases

Bags are an excellent choice when the structure of the data is unknown or otherwise not consistent. Some of the common use cases are as follows:

- Grouping together a bunch of `dask.delayed` calls—for example, for loading "messy" or unstructured (or unsupported) data.
- "Cleaning" (or adding structure to) unstructured data (like JSON).
- Parallelizing a group of tasks over a fixed range—for example, if you want to call an API 100 times but you are not picky about the details.
- Catch-all: if the data doesn't fit in any other collection type, bags are your friend.

We believe that the most common use case for Dask bags is loading messy data or data that Dask does not have built-in support for.

Loading and Saving Dask Bags

Dask bags have built-in readers for text files, with `read_text`, and avro files, with `read_avro`. Similarly, you can write Dask bags to text files and avro files, although the results must be serializable. Bags are commonly used when Dask's built-in tools for reading data are not enough, so the next section will dive into how to go beyond these two built-in formats.

Loading Messy Data with a Dask Bag

Normally, the goal when loading messy data is to get it into a structured format for further processing, or at least to extract the components that you are interested in. While your data formats will likely be a bit different, this section will look at loading some messy JSON and then extracting some relevant fields. Don't worry—we call out places where different formats or sources may require different techniques.

For messy textual data, which is a common occurrence with JSON, you can save yourself some time by loading the data using bags' `read_text` function. The `read_text` function defaults to splitting up the records by line; however, many formats cannot be processed by line. To get each whole file in a whole record rather than it being split up, you can set the `linedelimiter` parameter to one not found. Often REST APIs will return the results as a subcomponent, so in Example 5-1, we load the US Food and Drug Administration (FDA) recall dataset (*https://oreil.ly/3Xmd_*)

and strip it down to the part we care about. The FDA recall dataset is a wonderful real-world example of nested datasets often found in JSON data, which can be hard to process directly in DataFrames.

Example 5-1. Pre-processing JSON

```
def make_url(idx):
    page_size = 100
    start = idx * page_size
    u = f"https://api.fda.gov/food/enforcement.json?limit={page_size}&skip={start}"
    return u
```

```
urls = list(map(make_url, range(0, 10)))
# Since they are multi-line json we can't use the default \n line delim
raw_json = bag.read_text(urls, linedelimiter="NODELIM")
```

```
def clean_records(raw_records):
    import json
    # We don't need the meta field just the results field
    return json.loads(raw_records)["results"]
```

```
cleaned_records = raw_json.map(clean_records).flatten()
# And now we can convert it to a DataFrame
df = bag.Bag.to_dataframe(cleaned_records)
```

If you need to load data from an unsupported source (like a custom storage system) or a binary format (like protocol buffers or Flexible Image Transport System), you'll need to use lower-level APIs. For binary files that are still stored in an FSSPEC-supported filesystem like S3, you can try the pattern in Example 5-2.

Example 5-2. Loading PDFs from an FSSPEC-supported filesystem

```
def discover_files(path: str):
    (fs, fspath) = fsspec.core.url_to_fs(path)
    return (fs, fs.expand_path(fspath, recursive="true"))
```

```
def load_file(fs, file):
    """Load (and initially process) the data."""
    from PyPDF2 import PdfReader
    try:
        file_contents = fs.open(file)
        pdf = PdfReader(file_contents)
        return (file, pdf.pages[0].extract_text())
    except Exception as e:
        return (file, e)
```

```
def load_data(path: str):
    (fs, files) = discover_files(path)
    bag_filenames = bag.from_sequence(files)
    contents = bag_filenames.map(lambda f: load_file(fs, f))
    return contents
```

If you are not using a FSSPEC-supported filesystem, you can still load the data as illustrated in Example 5-3.

Example 5-3. Loading data using a purely custom function

```
def special_load_function(x):
    ## Do your special loading logic in this function, like reading a database
    return ["Timbit", "Is", "Awesome"][0: x % 4]


partitions = bag.from_sequence(range(20), npartitions=5)
raw_data = partitions.map(special_load_function).flatten()
```

 Loading data in this fashion requires that each file be able to fit inside a worker/executor. If that is not the case, things get much more complicated. Implementing splittable data readers is beyond the scope of this book, but you can take a look at Dask's internal IO libraries (text is the easiest) to get some inspiration.

Sometimes with nested directory structures, creating the list of files can take a long time. In that case, it's worthwhile to parallelize the listing of files as well. There are a number of different techniques to parallelize file listing, but for simplicity, we show parallel recursive listing in Example 5-4.

Example 5-4. Listing the files in parallel (recursively)

```
def parallel_recursive_list(path: str, fs=None) -> List[str]:
    print(f"Listing {path}")
    if fs is None:
        (fs, path) = fsspec.core.url_to_fs(path)
    info = []
    infos = fs.ls(path, detail=True)
    # Above could throw PermissionError, but if we can't list the dir it's
    # probably wrong so let it bubble up
    files = []
    dirs = []
    for i in infos:
        if i["type"] == "directory":
            # You can speed this up by using futures; covered in Chapter 6
            dir_list = dask.delayed(parallel_recursive_list)(i["name"], fs=fs)
```

```
        dirs += dir_list
    else:
        files.append(i["name"])
for sub_files in dask.compute(dirs):
    files.extend(sub_files)
return files
```

 You don't always have to do the directory listing yourself. It can be worthwhile to check whether there is a metastore, such as Hive or Iceberg, which can give you the list of files without all of these slow API calls.

This approach has some downsides: namely, all the filenames come back to a single point—but this is rarely an issue. However, if even just the list of your files is too big to fit in memory, you'll want to try a recursive algorithm for directory discovery, followed by an iterative algorithm for file listing that keeps the names of the files in the bag.[2] The code becomes a bit more complex, as shown in Example 5-5, so this last approach is rarely used.

Example 5-5. Listing the files in parallel without collecting to the driver

```
def parallel_list_directories_recursive(path: str, fs=None) -> List[str]:
    """
    Recursively find all the sub-directories.
    """
    if fs is None:
        (fs, path) = fsspec.core.url_to_fs(path)
    info = []
    # Ideally, we could filter for directories here, but fsspec lacks that (for
    # now)
    infos = fs.ls(path, detail=True)
    # Above could throw PermissionError, but if we can't list the dir, it's
    # probably wrong, so let it bubble up
    dirs = []
    result = []
    for i in infos:
        if i["type"] == "directory":
            # You can speed this up by using futures; covered in Chapter 6
            result.append(i["name"])
            dir_list = dask.delayed(
                parallel_list_directories_recursive)(i["name"], fs=fs)
            dirs += dir_list
    for sub_dirs in dask.compute(dirs):
        result.extend(sub_dirs)
    return result
```

---

2 Iterative algorithms involve using constructs like *while* or *for* instead of recursive calls to the same function.

```
def list_files(path: str, fs=None) -> List[str]:
    """List files at a given depth with no recursion."""
    if fs is None:
        (fs, path) = fsspec.core.url_to_fs(path)
    info = []
    # Ideally, we could filter for directories here, but fsspec lacks that (for
    # now)
    return map(lambda i: i["name"], filter(
        lambda i: i["type"] == "directory", fs.ls(path, detail=True)))


def parallel_list_large(path: str, npartitions=None, fs=None) -> bag:
    """
    Find all of the files (potentially too large to fit on the head node).
    """
    directories = parallel_list_directories_recursive(path, fs=fs)
    dir_bag = dask.bag.from_sequence(directories, npartitions=npartitions)
    return dir_bag.map(lambda dir: list_files(dir, fs=fs)).flatten()
```

A fully iterative algorithm with FSSPEC would not be any faster than the naive listing, since FSSPEC does not support querying just for directories.

Limitations

Dask bags are not well suited to most reduction or shuffling operations, as their core reduction function reduces results down to one partition, requiring that all of the data fit on a single machine. You can reasonably use aggregations that are purely constant space, such as mean, min, and max. However, most of the time you find yourself trying to aggregate your data, you should consider transforming your bag into a DataFrame with bag.Bag.to_dataframe.

 All three Dask data types (bag, array, and DataFrame) have methods for being converted to other data types. However, some conversions require special attention. For example, when converting a Dask DataFrame to a Dask array, the resulting array will have NaN if you look at the shape it generates. This is because Dask DataFrame does not keep track of the number of rows in each DataFrame chunk.

Conclusion

While Dask DataFrames get the most use, Dask arrays and bags have their place. You can use Dask arrays to speed up and parallelize large multi-dimensional array processes. Dask bags allow you to work with data that doesn't fit nicely into a DataFrame, like PDFs or multi-dimensional nested data. These collections get much less focus and active development than Dask DataFrames but may still have their place in your workflows. In the next chapter, you will see how you can add state to your Dask programs, including with operations on Dask's collections.

## CHAPTER 6

Advanced Task Scheduling: Futures and Friends

Dask's computational flow follows these four main logical steps, which can happen concurrently and recursively for each task:

1. Collect and read the input data.

2. Define and build the compute graph representing the set of computations that needs to be performed on the data.

3. Run the computation (this happens when you run `.compute()`).

4. Pass the result as data to the next step.

Now we introduce more ways to control this flow with futures. So far, you have mostly seen lazy operations in Dask, where Dask doesn't do the work until something forces the computation. This pattern has a number of benefits, including allowing Dask's optimizer to combine steps when doing so makes sense. However, not all tasks are well suited to lazy evaluation. One common pattern not well suited to lazy evaluation is *fire-and-forget*, where we call a function for its side effect[1] and necessarily care about the output. Trying to express this with lazy evaluation (e.g., `dask.delayed`) results in unnecessary blocking to force computation. When lazy evaluation is not what you need, you can explore Dask's futures. Futures can be used for much more than just fire-and-forget, and you can return results from them. This chapter will explore a number of common use cases for futures.

---

1 Like writing a file to disk or updating a database record.

You may already be familiar with futures from Python. Dask's futures are an extension of Python's concurrent.futures library, allowing you to use them in its place. Similar to using Dask Data-Frames in place of pandas DataFrames, the behavior can be a bit different (although the differences here are smaller).

Dask futures are a part of Dask's distributed client library, so you will get started by importing it with `from dask.distributed import Client`.

 Despite the name, you can use Dask's distributed client locally. Refer to "Distributed (Dask Client and Scheduler)" on page 19 for different local deployment types.

Lazy and Eager Evaluation Revisited

Eager evaluation is the most common form of evaluation in programming, including in Python. While most eager evaluation is blocking—that is, the program will not move to the next statement until the result is completed—you can still have asynchronous/non-blocking eager evaluation. Futures are one way of representing non-blocking eager computation.

Non-blocking eager evaluation still has some potential downsides compared to lazy evaluation. Some of these challenges include:

- The inability to combine adjacent stages (sometimes known as pipelining)
- Unnecessary computation:
  — Repeated subgraphs cannot be detected by Dask's optimizer.
  — Even if nothing depends on the result of the future, it may be computed.[2]
- Potential excessive blocking when futures launch and block on other futures
- A need for more careful memory management

Not all Python code is eagerly evaluated. In Python 3 some built-in functions use lazy evaluation, with operators like `map` returning iterators and evaluating elements only on request.

---

2 Although if the only reference to it gets garbage collected, it may not.

Use Cases for Futures

Many common use cases can be made faster with careful application of futures:

Integrating with other async servers (like Tornado)
> Although we generally believe that most of the time Dask is not the right solution for the "hot path," there are exceptions, such as dynamically computed analytic dashboards.

Request/response pattern
> Make a call to a remote service and (later) block on its result. This can include querying services like databases, remote procedure calls, or even websites.

IO
> Input/output can often be slow, but you know you want them to start happening as soon as possible.

Timeouts
> Sometimes you care about a result only if you can get it within a certain period of time. For example, think of a boosted ML model where you need to make a decision within a certain time frame, collecting all scores from available models quickly and then skipping any that take too long.

Fire-and-forget
> Sometimes you might not care about the result of a function call, but you do want to ensure it is called. Futures allow you to ensure a computation occurs without having to block on the result.

Actors
> The results from calling actors are futures. We cover actors in the next chapter.

Launching futures in Dask is non-blocking, whereas computing tasks in Dask is blocking. This means that when you submit a future to Dask, while it begins work right away, it does not stop (or block) your program from continuing.

Launching Futures

The syntax for launching Dask futures is a little different than that for `dask.delayed`. Dask futures are launched from the Dask distributed client with either `submit` for single futures or `map` for multiple futures, as shown in Example 6-1.

Example 6-1. Launching futures

```
from dask.distributed import Client
client = Client()


def slow(x):
    time.sleep(3 * x)
    return 3 * x


slow_future = client.submit(slow, 1)
slow_futures = client.map(slow, range(1, 5))
```

Unlike with `dask.delayed`, as soon as the future is launched, Dask begins to compute the value.

 While this map is somewhat similar to the map on Dask bags, each item results in a separate task, whereas bags are able to group together tasks into partitions to reduce the overhead (although they are lazily evaluated).

Some actions in Dask, like `persist()` on Dask collections, use futures under the hood. You can get the futures of the persisted collection by calling `futures_of`. These futures follow the same life cycle as the futures that you launch yourself.

Future Life Cycle

Futures have a different life cycle from `dask.delayed` beyond eager computation. With `dask.delayed`, intermediate computations are automatically cleaned up; however, Dask futures results are stored until either the future is explicitly canceled or the reference to it is garbage collected in Python. If you no longer need the value of a future, you can cancel it and free any storage space or cores used by calling `.cancel`. The future life cycle is illustrated in Example 6-2.

Example 6-2. Future life cycle

```
myfuture = client.submit(slow, 5) # Starts running
myfuture = None # future may be GCd and then stop since there are no other references

myfuture = client.submit(slow, 5) # Starts running
del myfuture # future may be GCd and then stop since there are no other references

myfuture = client.submit(slow, 5) # Starts running
# Future stops running, any other references point to canceled future
myfuture.cancel()
```

Canceling a future behaves differently than deleting or depending on garbage collection. If there is another reference to the future, then deleting or setting the individual reference to None will not cancel the future. This means the result will remain stored in Dask. On the other hand, canceling futures has the downside that if you are incorrect and the futures value is needed, this will cause an error.

 When using Dask in a Jupyter notebook, the notebook may "hold on to" the result of any previous cell, so even if the future is unnamed, it will remain present in Dask. There is a discussion on Discourse (*https://oreil.ly/zyy2H*) with more context for those interested.

The string representation of a future will show you where it is in its life cycle (e.g., `Future: slow status: cancelled,`).

Fire-and-Forget

Sometimes you no longer need a future, but you also don't want it to be canceled. This pattern is called fire-and-forget. This is most useful for things like writing data out, updating a database, or other side effects. If all reference to a future is lost, garbage collection can result in the future being canceled. To work around this, Dask has the aptly named `fire_and_forget` method, which allows you to take advantage of this pattern, as shown in Example 6-3, without needing to keep references around.

Example 6-3. Fire-and-forget

```
from dask.distributed import fire_and_forget


def do_some_io(data):
    """
    Do some io we don't need to block on :)
    """
    import requests
    return requests.get('https://httpbin.org/get', params=data)


def business_logic():
    # Make a future, but we don't really care about its result, just that it
    # happens
    future = client.submit(do_some_io, {"timbit": "awesome"})
    fire_and_forget(future)


business_logic()
```

Retrieving Results

More commonly, you will eventually want to know what the future has computed (or even just if it encountered an error). For futures that are not just side effects, you'll eventually want to get the return value (or error) from the futures. Futures have the blocking method `result`, as shown in Example 6-4, which gives you back the value computed in the future or raises the exception from the future.

Example 6-4. Getting the result

```
future = client.submit(do_some_io, {"timbit": "awesome"})
future.result()
```

You can extend this to multiple futures, as in Example 6-5, but there are ways to do it faster.

Example 6-5. Getting a list of results

```
for f in futures:
    time.sleep(2) # Business numbers logic
    print(f.result())
```

If you've got multiple futures together—say, you created them with `map`—you can get the results back as they become available (see Example 6-6). If you can process the results out of order, this can greatly improve your processing time.

Example 6-6. Getting a list of results as they become available

```
from dask.distributed import as_completed

for f in as_completed(futures):
    time.sleep(2) # Business numbers logic
    print(f.result())
```

In the preceding example, by processing futures as they complete you can have the main thread do its "business logic" (similar to `combine` step for an aggregate) for each element as it becomes available. If the futures finish at different times, this can be a large speed increase.

If you have a deadline, like scoring a model for ad serving[3] or doing something funky with the stock market, you might not want to wait for all of your futures. Instead, the wait function allows you to fetch results with a timeout, as shown in Example 6-7.

Example 6-7. Getting the first future (within a time limit)

```
from dask.distributed import wait
from dask.distributed.client import FIRST_COMPLETED

# Will throw an exception if no future completes in time.
# If it does not throw, the result has two lists:
# The done list may return between one and all futures.
# The not_done list may contain zero or more futures.
finished = wait(futures, 1, return_when=FIRST_COMPLETED)

# Process the returned futures
for f in finished.done:
    print(f.result())

# Cancel the futures we don't need
for f in finished.not_done:
    f.cancel()
```

This time limit can apply either to the entire set or to one future at a time. If you want all features finished by a given time, then you need a bit more work, as shown in Example 6-8.

Example 6-8. Getting any futures that finish within a time limit

```
max_wait = 10
start = time.time()

while len(futures) > 0 and time.time() - start < max_wait:
    try:
        finished = wait(futures, 1, return_when=FIRST_COMPLETED)
        for f in finished.done:
            print(f.result())
        futures = finished.not_done
    except TimeoutError:
        True # No future finished in this cycle

# Cancel any remaining futures
for f in futures:
    f.cancel()
```

---

3 We believe that this is one of the areas in which Dask has more room for growth, and if you do want to implement a microservice for deadline-critical events, you may want to explore using Dask in conjunction with other systems, like Ray.

Now that you can get the results from futures, you can compare the execution time of dask.delayed versus Dask futures, as shown in Example 6-9.

Example 6-9. Seeing that futures can be faster

```
slow_future = client.submit(slow, 1)
slow_delayed = dask.delayed(slow)(1)
# Pretend we do some other work here
time.sleep(1)
future_time = timeit.timeit(lambda: slow_future.result(), number=1)
delayed_time = timeit.timeit(lambda: dask.compute(slow_delayed), number=1)
print(
    f"""So as you can see by the future time {future_time} v.s. {delayed_time}
    the future starts running right away."""
)
```

In this (albeit contrived) example, you can see how, by starting the work as soon as possible, the future is completed by the time you get the result, whereas the dask.delayed starts only when you get there.

Nested Futures

As with dask.delayed, you can also launch futures from inside futures. The syntax is a bit different, as you need to get an instance of the client object, which is not serializable, so dask.distributed has the special function get_client to get the client inside a distributed function. Once you have the client, you can then launch the future like normal, as shown in Example 6-10.

Example 6-10. Launching a nested future

```
from dask.distributed import get_client


def nested(x):
    client = get_client() # The client is serializable, so we use get_client
    futures = client.map(slow, range(0, x))
    r = 0
    for f in as_completed(futures):
        r = r + f.result()
    return r


f = client.submit(nested, 3)
f.result()
```

Note that since Dask uses a centralized scheduler, the client is communicating with that centralized scheduler to determine where to place the future.

Distributed Data Structures for Scheduling

Dask also has a collection of data structures to simplify task coordination. These data structures include queues, locks/semaphores, events, and publish/subscriber topics. These distributed data structures aim to behave similarly to their local counterparts, but it's important to remember that the distributed nature of Dask adds overhead for coordination and remote procedure calls.

For example, Dask's distributed variable is called `Variable`, which implements `get`, `set`, and `delete`. The `get` function takes a `timeout`, which should remind you that these operations are distributed in nature and therefore are slower than updating a local variable. As with multi-threaded global variables, race conditions can occur when different workers update the same local variable.

 You can name Dask's distributed data structures when constructing them, and two resources with the same name will be resolved to the same object even if they are constructed separately.

Conclusion

While Dask's primary building block is `dask.delayed`, it's not the only option. You can control more of your execution flow by using Dask's futures. Futures are ideal for I/O, model inference, and deadline-sensitive applications. In exchange for this additional control, you are responsible for managing the life cycle of your futures and the data they produce in a way that you are not with `dask.delayed`. Dask also has a number of distributed data structures, including queues, variables, and locks. While these distributed data structures are more expensive than their local counterparts, they also give you another layer of flexibility around controlling your task scheduling.

## CHAPTER 7

Adding Changeable/Mutable State with Dask Actors

Dask is focused on scaling analytic use cases, but you can use it to scale many other types of problems. So far, most of the tools you have used in Dask are functional. Functional programming means that previous calls do not impact future calls. Stateless functions are common in distributed systems like Dask, as they can safely be re-executed multiple times on failure. Updating the weights of a model during training is an example of state common in data science. One of the most common ways of handling state in a distributed system is with the actor model. This chapter will introduce both the general actor model and Dask's specific implementation.

Dask futures offer a non-mutable distributed state, where values are stored on the workers. However, this doesn't work well for situations in which you want to update the state, like changing a bank account balance (an alternative solution is illustrated in Example 7-1), or updating machine learning model weights during training.

Dask actors have a number of limitations, and we believe that in many cases the right answer is to keep mutable state *outside* of Dask (like in a database).

Of course, you don't have to use distributed mutable state. In some cases, you may choose to not use distributed state and instead put it all in your main program. This can quickly lead to bottlenecks on the node responsible for your main program. Other options include storing your state outside of Dask, like in a database, which has its own trade-offs. While this chapter focuses on how to use the actor model, we conclude with when not to use Dask actors and alternatives for handling state, which is of equal importance.

Dask also has distributed mutable objects, covered in "Distributed Data Structures for Scheduling" on page 79.

What Is the Actor Model?

In the actor model, actors do the following:

- Store data
- Receive and respond to messages, including from other actors and external
- Pass messages
- Create new actors

The actor model is a technique of dealing with state in parallel and distributed systems that avoid locks. While proper locking ensures that only one piece of code modifies a given value, it can be very expensive and difficult to get right. A common problem with locking is known as deadlocking—this is where resources are acquired/released in an incorrect order that the program can block forever. The slowness and difficulty of locks only increase in distributed systems.[1] The actor model was introduced in 1973 and has since been implemented in most programming languages,[2] with some popular modern implementations including Akka in Scala and the .NET languages.

It can be helpful to think of each actor as a person holding a note about their state, and that person is the only one allowed to read or update the note. Whenever another part of the code wants to access or modify the state, it must ask the actor to do this.

Conceptually, this is very similar to classes in object-oriented programming. However, unlike with generic classes, actors process one request at a time to ensure an actor's state consistency. To improve the throughput, people often create a pool of actors (assuming they can shard or replicate the actor's state). We'll cover an example in the next section.

The actor model is a good fit for many distributed systems scenarios. Here are some typical use cases in which the actor model can be advantageous:

---

1 See the ZooKeeper documentation (*https://oreil.ly/btzJK*) for an understanding of ZooKeeper's distributed performance.

2 The actor model was extended in 1985 for concurrent computation; see "Actors: A Model of Concurrent Computation in Distributed Systems" (*https://oreil.ly/uPCfx*) by Gul Abdulnabi Agha.

- You need to deal with a large distributed state that is hard to synchronize between invocations (e.g., ML model weights, counters, etc.).

- You want to work with single-threaded objects that do not require significant interaction from external components. This is especially useful for legacy code that is not fully understood.[3]

Now that you have an understanding of the actor model in general, it's time for you to learn about how Dask implements it, and about its trade-offs.

Dask Actors

Dask actors are one implementation of actors, and some of the properties differ between Dask and other systems. Unlike the rest of Dask, Dask actors are not resilient to failures. If the node, or process, running the actor fails, the data inside the actor is lost and Dask is not able to recover from it.

Your First Actor (It's a Bank Account)

Creating an actor in Dask is relatively simple. To start with, you make a normal Python class with functions that you will call. These functions are responsible for receiving and responding to messages in the actor model. Once you have your class, you submit it to Dask, along with the flag actor=True, and Dask gives you back a future representing a reference to the actor. When you get the result of this future, Dask creates and returns to you a proxy object, which passes any function calls as messages to the actor.

> Note this is effectively an object-oriented bank account implementation, except we don't have any locks since we only ever have a single thread changing the values.

Let's take a look at how you can implement a common example actor for a bank account. In Example 7-1, we define three methods—balance, deposit, and withdrawal—that can be used to interact with the actor. Once the actor is defined, we ask Dask to schedule the actor so that we can call it.

---

3 Think COBOL, where the author left and the documentation was lost, but when you tried to turn it off accounting came running, literally.

Example 7-1. Making a bank account actor

```
class BankAccount:
    """ A bank account actor (similar to counter but with + and -)"""

    # 42 is a good start
    def __init__(self, balance=42.0):
        self._balance = balance

    def deposit(self, amount):
        if amount < 0:
            raise Exception("Cannot deposit negative amount")
        self._balance += amount
        return self._balance

    def withdrawal(self, amount):
        if amount > self._balance:
            raise Exception("Please deposit more money first.")
        self._balance -= amount
        return self._balance

    def balance(self):
        return self._balance


# Create a BankAccount on a worker
account_future = client.submit(BankAccount, actor=True)
account = account_future.result()
```

When you call methods on the resulting proxy object (see Example 7-2), Dask dispatches a remote procedure call and returns a special ActorFuture immediately. This allows you to use actors in a non-blocking fashion. Unlike the generic @dask.delayed calls, these are all routed to the same process, namely the one where Dask has scheduled the actor.

Example 7-2. Using the bank account actor

```
# Non-blocking
balance_future = account.balance()
# Blocks
balance = balance_future.result()
try:
    f = account.withdrawal(100)
    f.result() # throws an exception
except Exception as e:
    print(e)
```

The ActorFuture *is not serializable*, so if you need to transfer the result of calling an actor, you need to block and get its value, as shown in Example 7-3.

Example 7-3. ActorFutures are not serializable

```
def inc(x):
    import time
    time.sleep(x)
    f = counter.add(x)
    # Note: the actor (in this case `counter`) is serializable;
    # however, the future we get back from it is not.
    # This is likely because the future contains a network connection
    # to the actor, so need to get its concrete value here. If we don't
    # need the value, you can avoid blocking and it will still execute.
    return f.result()
```

While having one actor per bank account does a good job of avoiding bottlenecks, since each bank account likely won't have too many transactions queued, it is slightly inefficient, as there is a non-zero actor overhead. One solution is to extend our bank account actor to support multiple accounts by using a key and hashmap, but if all accounts are inside one actor, this can lead to scaling problems.

Scaling Dask Actors

The actor model described earlier in this chapter typically assumes that actors are lightweight, meaning they contain a single piece of state, and do not require scaling/parallelization. In Dask and similar systems (including Akka), actors are often used for coarser-grained implementations and can require scaling.[4]

As with dask.delayed, you can scale actors horizontally (across processes/machines) by creating multiple actors or vertically (with more resources). Scaling actors horizontally is not as simple as just adding more machines or workers, since Dask cannot break up a single actor across multiple processes.

When scaling actors horizontally, it is up to you to break up the state in such a way that you can have multiple actors handling it. One technique is to use *actor pools* (see Figure 7-1). These pools can have a static mapping of, say, user → actor, or, in the situation in which the actors share a database, round-robin or other non-deterministic balancing can be used.

---

4 A *coarse-grained* actor is one that may contain multiple pieces of state; a *fine-grained* actor is one where each piece of state would be represented as a separate actor. This is similar to the concept of coarse-grained locking (*https://oreil.ly/7RMkS*).

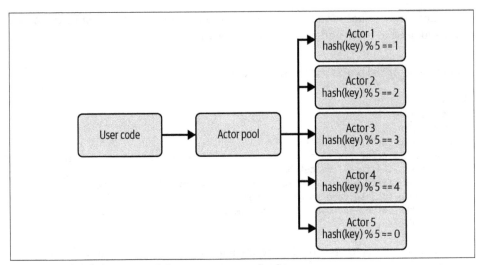

Figure 7-1. Scaled actor model using consistent hashing

We extend the bank account example to a "bank" where an actor may be responsible for multiple accounts (but not for all of the accounts in the bank). We can then use an actor pool with hashing to route the requests to the correct "branch" or actor, as shown in Example 7-4.

Example 7-4. Hashing actor pool example for a bank

```
class SketchyBank:
    """ A sketchy bank (handles multiple accounts in one actor)."""

    # 42 is a good start
    def __init__(self, accounts={}):
        self._accounts = accounts

    def create_account(self, key):
        if key in self._accounts:
            raise Exception(f"{key} is already an account.")
        self._accounts[key] = 0.0

    def deposit(self, key, amount):
        if amount < 0:
            raise Exception("Cannot deposit negative amount")
        if key not in self._accounts:
            raise Exception(f"Could not find account {key}")
        self._accounts[key] += amount
        return self._accounts[key]

    def withdrawal(self, key, amount):
        if key not in self._accounts:
            raise Exception(f"Could not find account {key}")
```

```python
        if amount > self._accounts[key]:
            raise Exception("Please deposit more money first.")
        self._accounts[key] -= amount
        return self._accounts[key]

    def balance(self, key):
        if key not in self._accounts:
            raise Exception(f"Could not find account {key}")
        return self._accounts[key]


class HashActorPool:
    """A basic deterministic actor pool."""

    def __init__(self, actorClass, num):
        self._num = num
        # Make the request number of actors
        self._actors = list(
            map(lambda x: client.submit(SketchyBank, actor=True).result(),
                range(0, num)))

    def actor_for_key(self, key):
        return self._actors[hash(key) % self._num]


holdens_questionable_bank = HashActorPool(SketchyBank, 10)
holdens_questionable_bank.actor_for_key("timbit").create_account("timbit")
holdens_questionable_bank.actor_for_key(
    "timbit").deposit("timbit", 42.0).result()
```

Limitations

As previously mentioned, Dask actors are not resilient to machine or process failure. This is a design decision in Dask and is not true for all actor systems. Many, but not all, actor systems offer different options for the persistence and recovery of actors during failure. For example, Ray has the concept of recoverable actors (managed automatically inside of workflows or manually).

 Calls to dask.delayed functions may be retried on failure, and if they call functions on actors, those function calls will then be duplicated. If you cannot have a function replayed, then you need to ensure it is called only from inside other actors.

Dask's actor model is less full-featured than Ray's actor model, much as Ray's Data-Frame is less full-featured than Dask's. You may wish to consider running Dask on Ray to get the best of both worlds. While Holden is biased, she suggests you check out her book *Scaling Python with Ray* if you are interested in Ray.

When to Use Dask Actors

A common problem in the industry is not realizing when our cool new tool is not the right tool for the job. As the saying goes, "When you have a hammer, the whole world looks like a nail." *You likely do not need actors and should stick with tasks if you are not mutating state.* It is important for you to remember that there are other options for handling state, as shown in Table 7-1.

Table 7-1. Comparison of techniques for managing mutable state

	Local state (e.g., driver)	Dask actors	External distributed state (e.g., ZooKeeper, Ray, or AKKA)
Scalability	No, all state must fit on a single machine.	State within each actor must fit on a machine, but actors are spread out.	Yes[a]
Resilience	Medium, but no increase in resilience cost (e.g., loss of driver is already catastrophic)	No, loss of any worker with an actor becomes catastrophic.	Yes, loss of entire cluster can be recovered from.
Performance overhead	RPC to driver	Same as dask.delayed	RPC to external system + external systems overhead
Code complexity	Low	Medium	High (new library to learn and integrate), extra logic for avoiding duplicate execution
Deployment complexity	Low	Low	High (new system to maintain)

[a] Ray actors still require that the state within an actor must fit on a single machine. Ray has additional tools to shard or create pools of actors.

As with most things in life, picking the right technique is a compromise specific to the problem you are trying to solve. We believe that one of the two local (e.g., driver) states, or the use of Ray actors in conjunction with Dask for its analytical powers, can handle most cases in which you need mutable state.

Conclusion

In this chapter you have learned the basics of how the actor model works as well as how Dask implements it. You've also learned some alternatives for dealing with state in a distributed system, and how to choose between them. Dask actors are a relatively new part of Dask and do not have the same resilience properties as delayed functions. The failure of a worker containing an actor cannot be recovered from. Many other actor systems offer some ability to recover from failures, and if you find yourself depending heavily on actors, you may wish to explore alternatives.

## CHAPTER 8

How to Evaluate Dask's Components and Libraries

It's hard, although possible, to build reliable systems out of unreliable components.[1] Dask is a largely community-driven open source project, and its components evolve at different rates. Not all parts of Dask are equally mature; even the components we cover in this book have different levels of support and development. While Dask's core parts are well maintained and tested, some parts lack the same level of maintenance.

Still, there are already dozens of popular libraries specifically for Dask, and the open source Dask community is growing around them. This gives us some confidence that many of these libraries are here to stay. Table 8-1 shows a non-exhaustive list of foundational libraries in use and their relation to the core Dask project. It is meant as a road map for users and is not an endorsement of individual projects. Though we haven't attempted to cover all the projects shown here, we offer evaluation of some individual projects throughout the book.

---

1 Although, in many ways, distributed systems have evolved to overcome their unreliable components. For example, fault tolerance is something a single machine cannot achieve but distributed systems can accomplish with replication.

Table 8-1. Libraries frequently used with Dask

Category	Subcategory	Libraries
Dask project		• Dask • Distributed • dask-ml
Data structures: Extend functionality, specific scientific data handling, or deployment hardware options of Dask built-in data structures	Functionalities and convenience	• *xarray*: adds axis labels for Dask array • *sparse*: an efficient implementation for sparse arrays and matrices, often found in ML and deep learning • *pint*: scientific unit conversion • *dask-geopandas*: parallelization of geopandas
	Hardware	• *RAPIDS project*: NVIDIA-led effort to extend CUDA data structure for Dask • *dask-cuda*:[a] provides CUDA cluster, an extension of Dask's cluster that better manages CUDA-enabled Dask workers • *cuPY*:[a] GPU-enabled arrays • *cuDF*:[a] CUDA DataFrame as partitions in Dask DataFrame
Deployment: Extend deployment options for use with Dask distributed	Containers	• *dask-kubernetes*:[a] Dask on k8s • *dask-helm*:[a] alternate Dask on k8s and jupyterhub on k8s
	Cloud	• *dask-cloudprovider*: commodity cloud APIs • *dask-gateway* • *Dask-Yarn*:[a] for YARN/Hadoop
	GPU	• *dask-cuda*: Dask cluster optimized for GPUs
	HPC	• *Dask-jobqueue*:[a] deployment for PBS, Slurm, MOAB, SGE, LSF, and HTCondor • *dask-mpi*:[a] deployment for MPI
ML and analytics: Extend ML libraries and computation with Dask		• *dask-ml*:[a] Distributed implementation of scikit-learn and more • *xgboost*:[a] gradient boosting with native Dask support • *light-gbm*:[a] another tree-based learning algorithm with native Dask support • *Dask-SQL*:[a] CPU-based SQL engine for Dask (ETL/compute logic can be run on SQL context; similar to SparkSQL) • *BlazingSQL*:[a] SQL query on cuDF and Dask • *FugueSQL*:[a] portability between pandas, Dask, and Spark, using the same SQL code (downside: requires ANTLR, a JVM-based tool) • *Dask-on-Ray*:[a] Dask's distributed data structures and task graphs, run on Ray scheduler

[a] Covered in this book.

It's essential to understand the state of the components that you are considering using. If you need to use a less maintained or developed part of Dask, defensive programming (*https://oreil.ly/IDXVs*), including thorough code testing, will become even more critical. Working on less-established parts of the Dask ecosystem can also be an exciting opportunity to become more involved and contribute fixes or documentation.

 This is not to say that closed source software does not suffer from the same challenges (e.g., untested components), but we are in a better place to evaluate and make informed choices with open source software.

Of course, not all of our projects need to be maintainable, but as the saying goes, "Nothing is more permanent than a temporary fix." If something is truly a one-time-use project, you can likely skip most of the analysis here and try out the libraries to see if they work for you.

Dask is under rapid development, and any static table of which components are production-ready would be out of date by the time it was read. So instead of sharing our views on which components of Dask are currently well developed, this chapter aims to give you the tools to evaluate the libraries you may be considering. In this chapter, we separate metrics that you can measure concretely from the fuzzier qualitative metrics. Perhaps counterintuitively, we believe that the "fuzzier" qualitative metrics are a better framework for evaluating components and projects.

Along the way, we'll look at some projects and how they are measured, but please keep in mind that these specific observations may be out of date by the time you read this, and you should do your own evaluation with the tools provided here.

 While we focus on the Dask ecosystem in this chapter, you can apply most of these techniques throughout software tool selection.

Qualitative Considerations for Project Evaluation

We start by focusing on qualitative tools since we believe these tools are the best for determining the suitability of a particular library for your project.

Project Priorities

Some projects prioritize benchmarks or performance numbers, while other projects can prioritize correctness and clarity, and still others may prioritize completeness. A project's README or home page is often a good sign of what the project prioritizes. Early in its creation, Apache Spark's home page focused on performance with benchmarks, whereas now it shows an ecosystem of tools leading more toward completeness. The Dask Kubernetes GitHub README shows a collection of badges indicating the state of the code and not much else, revealing a strong developer focus.

While there are many arguments for and against focusing on benchmarks, correctness should almost never be sacrificed.[2] This does not mean that libraries will never have bugs; rather, projects should take reports of correctness issues seriously and treat them with higher priority than others. An excellent way to see whether a project values correctness is to look for reports of correctness and observe how the core developers respond.

Many Dask ecosystem projects use GitHub's built-in issue tracker, but if you don't see any activity, check the README and developer guides to see if the project uses a different issue tracker. For example, many ASF projects use JIRA. Looking into how folks respond to issues gives you a good idea of what issues they consider important. You don't need to look at all of them, but a small sample of 10 will often give you a good idea (look at open and not fixed issues as well as closed and fixed ones).

Community

As one of the unofficial ASF sayings goes, "Community over code."[3] The Apache Way website (*https://oreil.ly/CcJZ1*) describes this as meaning "the most successful long-lived projects value a broad and collaborative community over the details of the code itself." This saying matches our experience, in which we've found that technical improvements are easier to copy from other projects, but the community is much harder to move. Measuring community is challenging, and it can be tempting to look at the number of developers or users, but we think it's essential to go beyond that.

Finding the community associated with a particular project can be tricky. Take your time to look around at issue trackers, source code, forums (like Discourse), and mailing lists. For example, Dask's Discourse group (*https://oreil.ly/hSVE0*) is highly active. Some projects use IRC, Slack, or Discord, or their "interactive" communication—and in our opinion, some of the best projects put in the effort to make the conversations from these communication channels appear in search indexes. Sometimes parts of the community may exist on external social media sites, and these pose a unique set of challenges to community standards.

There are multiple types of communities for open source software projects. The user community is the people who are using the software to build things. The developer

---

2 Sacrificing correctness means producing incorrect results. An example correctness issue is set_index in Dask-on-Ray causing rows to disappear; this issue took about a month to fix, which in our opinion is quite reasonable given the challenges in reproducing it (*https://oreil.ly/P1L1W*). Sometimes correctness fixes, like security fixes, can result in slower processing; for example, MongoDB's defaults are very fast but can lose data.

3 We are uncertain of exactly whom or where this quote originates from; it's appeared in the ASF director's position statement as well as in the Apache Way documentation.

community is the group working on improving the library. Some projects have large intersections between these communities, but often the user community is much larger than the developer community. We are biased toward evaluating the developer community, but it's important to ensure both are healthy. Software projects without enough developers will move slowly, and projects without users are frequently challenging to use by anyone except the developers.

In many situations, a large community with enough jerks (or a lead jerk) can be a much less enjoyable environment than a small community of nice folks. You are less likely to be productive if you are not enjoying your work. Sadly, figuring out if someone is a jerk or if a community has jerks in it is a complex problem. If people are generally rude on the mailing list or in the issue tracker, this can be a sign that the community is not as welcoming to new members.[4]

Some projects, including one of Holden's projects, have attempted to quantify some of these metrics using sentiment analysis combined with random sampling (*https://oreil.ly/ZLJ63*), but this is a time-consuming process you can probably skip in most cases.

Even with the nicest people, it can matter which institutions the contributors are associated with. If, for example, the top contributors are all grad students in the same research lab or work at the same company, the risk that the software is abandoned increases. This is not to say that single-company or even single-person open source projects are bad,[5] but you should adjust your expectations to match.

If you are concerned a project does not meet your current level of maturity and you have a budget, this can be an excellent opportunity to support critical open source projects. Reach out to maintainers and see what they need; sometimes, it's as simple as writing them a check for new hardware or hiring them to provide training for your company.

Beyond whether people are nice in a community, it can be a positive sign if folks are using the project similarly to how you are considering using it. If, for example, you are the first person to apply Dask DataFrames to a new domain, even though Dask DataFrames themselves are very mature, you are more likely to find missing components than if other folks in the same area of application are already using Dask.

---

4 The Linux kernel is a classic example of a somewhat more challenging community (*https://oreil.ly/tXjhn*).

5 One example of a small community developing a very popular and successful project is homebrew.

Dask-Specific Best Practices

When it comes to Dask libraries, there are a number of Dask-specific best practices to look for. In general, libraries should not have too much work on the client node, and as much work as possible should be delegated to the workers. Sometimes the documentation will gloss over which parts happen where, and the fastest way to tell in our experience is to simply run the example code and look to see which tasks are getting scheduled on the workers. Relatedly, libraries should bring back only the smallest bits of data when possible. These best practices are slightly different from those for when you are writing your own Dask code, since you can know what your data size is beforehand and determine when local compute is the best path forward.

Up-to-Date Dependencies

If a project pins a dependency at a specific version, it is important that the version pinned does not have conflicts with the other packages you want to use and, even more importantly, does not have pinned insecure dependencies. What constitutes "up to date" is a matter of opinion. If you are the kind of developer who likes using the latest version of everything, you'll probably be happiest with libraries that (mostly) provide minimum but not maximum versions. However, this can be misleading as, especially in the Python ecosystem, many libraries do not use semantic versioning (*https://oreil.ly/RVVI7*)—including Dask, which uses CalVer (*https:// oreil.ly/fTTXZ*)—and just because a project does not exclude a new version does not mean it will actually work with it.

 Some folks would call this quantitative, but in a CalVer-focused ecosystem, we believe this is more qualitative.

A good check, when considering adding a new library to an existing environment, is to try to run the new libraries test suite in the virtual environment that you plan to use it in (or in an equivalently configured one).

Documentation

While not every tool needs a book (although we do hope you find books useful), very few libraries are truly self-explanatory. On the low end, for simple libraries, a few examples or well-written tests can serve as a stand-in for proper documentation. Complete documentation is a good sign of overall project maturity. Not all documentation is created equal, and as the saying goes, documentation is normally out of date as soon as it is finished (if not before). A good exercise to do, before you dive all the way into a new library, is to open up the documentation and try to run the examples.

If the getting-started examples don't work (and you can't figure out how to fix them), you will likely be in for a rough ride.

Sometimes good documentation exists but is separate from the project (e.g., in books), and some research may be required. If you find a project has good but not self-evident documentation, consider trying to improve the visibility of the documentation.

Openness to Contributions

If you find the library is promising but not all the way there, it's important to be able to contribute your improvements back to the library. This is good for the community, and besides, if you can't upstream your improvements, upgrading to new versions will be more challenging.[6] Many projects nowadays have contribution guides that can give you an idea of how they like to work, but nothing beats a real test contribution. A great place to start with a project is fixing its documentation with the eyes of a newcomer, especially those getting-started examples from the previous section. Documentation often becomes out of sync in fast-moving projects, and if you find it difficult to get your documentation changes accepted, that is a strong indicator of how challenging it will be to contribute more complicated improvements later.

Something to pay attention to is what the issue-reporting experience is like. Since almost no software is completely free of bugs, you may encounter an issue. Whether you have the energy or skills to fix the bug, sharing your experience is vital so it can be fixed. Sharing the bug can help the next person encountering the same challenge feel not alone, even if the issue is unresolved.

 Pay attention to your experience when trying to report an issue. Most large projects with active communities will have some guidance to help you submit your issue and ensure it's not duplicating a previous issue. If that guidance is lacking (or if the project has a smaller community associated with it), reporting an issue could be more challenging.

If you don't have time to make your own test contribution, you can always take a look at a project's pull requests (or equivalent) and see if the responses seem positive or antagonistic.

---

6 Changes from upstream open source that you are unable to contribute back mean that you need to reapply those changes every time you upgrade. While modern tools like Git simplify the mechanics of this a little bit, it can be a time-consuming process.

Extensibility

Not all changes to libraries necessarily need to be able to go upstream. If a library is appropriately structured, you can add additional functionality without changing the underlying code. Part of what makes Dask so powerful is its extensibility. For example, adding user-defined functions and aggregations allows Dask to be usable by many.

Quantitative Metrics for Open Source Project Evaluation

As software developers and data scientists, we often try to use quantitative metrics to make our decisions. Quantitative metrics for software, in both open source and closed source, is an area of active research, so we won't be able to cover all of the quantitative metrics. A large challenge with all of the quantitative metrics for open source projects is that, especially once money gets involved, the metrics can be influenced. We instead recommend focusing on qualitative factors, which, while more difficult to measure, are also more difficult to game.

Here we cover a few common metrics that folks commonly attempt to use, and there are many other frameworks for evaluating open source projects for use, including the OSSM (*https://oreil.ly/4lvK6*), OpenSSF Security Metrics (*https://oreil.ly/Pcioq*), and many more (*https://oreil.ly/6mmHu*). Some of these frameworks ostensibly produce automated scores (like the OpenSSF), but in our experience, not only are the metrics collected gameable, they are often collected incorrectly.[7]

Release History

Frequent releases can be a sign of a healthy library. If a project has not been released for a long time, you are more likely to run into conflicts with other libraries. For libraries built on top of tools like Dask, one detail to check is how many months (or days) it takes for a new version of the library to be released on top of the latest version of Dask. Some libraries do not do traditional releases, but rather suggest installing directly from the source repo. This is often a sign of a project earlier in the development phase, which can be more challenging to take on as a dependency.[8]

---

7 For example, the OpenSSF reports that Apache Spark has unsigned releases, but all of the releases are signed. Projects that are highly critical (like log4j) incorrectly have low criticality scores, illustrating some of the limits of these metrics.

8 In these cases it's good to pick a tag or a commit to install from so you don't end up with mismatched versions.

Release history is one of the easiest metrics to game, as all it requires is the developers making a release. Some development styles will automatically create releases after every successful check-in, which in our opinion is an anti-pattern,[9] as you often want some additional level of human testing or checking before a full release.

Commit Frequency (and Volume)

Another popular metric people consider is commit frequency or volume. This metric is far from perfect, as the frequency and volume can vary widely depending on coding styles, which lack correlation with software quality. For example, developers who tend to squash commits can have lower commit volume, whereas developers who use rebases primarily will have a higher volume of commits.

On the flip side, the complete lack of recent commits can be a sign that a project has become abandoned, and if you decide to use it, you will end up having to maintain a fork.

Library Usage

One of the simplest metrics to check is if people are using a package, which you can see by looking at the installs. You can check PyPI package install stats on the PyPI Stats website (*https://oreil.ly/1HHL8*) (see Figure 8-1) or on Google's BigQuery (*https://oreil.ly/83RIO*), and conda installs using the condastats library (*https://oreil.ly/4STsP*).

Unfortunately, installation counts are a noisy metric, as PyPI downloads can come from anything from CI pipelines to even someone spinning up a new cluster with the library installed but never used. Not only is this metric unintentionally noisy, but the same techniques can also be used to increase the numbers artificially.

Instead of depending heavily on the number of package installs, we like to see if we can find examples of people using the libraries—such as by searching for imports on GitHub or Sourcegraph (*https://oreil.ly/FrPTE*). For example, we can try to get an approximate number of people using Streamz or cuDF with Dask by searching (`file:requirements.txt OR file:setup.py) cudf AND dask` (*https://oreil.ly/gQWZY*) and `(file:requirements.txt OR file:setup.py) streamz AND dask` (*https://oreil.ly/tYIJu*) with Sourcegraph, which yields 72 and 33, respectively. This captures only a few, but when we compare this to the same query for Dask (which yields 500+), it suggests that Streamz has lower usage than cuDF in the Dask ecosystem.

---

9 Snapshot artifacts are OK.

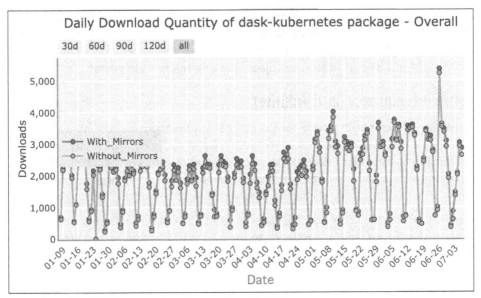

Figure 8-1. Dask Kubernetes install stats from PyPI Stats

Looking for examples of people using a library has its limitations, especially with data processing. Since data and machine learning pipelines are not as frequently open sourced, finding examples can be harder for libraries used for those purposes.

Another proxy for usage you can look at is the frequency of issues or mailing list posts. If a project is hosted on something like GitHub, stars can also be an interesting way of measuring usage—but since people can now buy GitHub stars just like Instagram likes (as shown in Figure 8-2), you shouldn't weigh this metric too heavily.[10]

Even setting aside people purchasing stars, what constitutes a project worth starring varies from person to person. Some projects will, while not purchasing stars, ask many individuals to star their projects, which can quickly inflate this metric.[11]

---

10 There are some tools that can help you dig deeper into the star data, including ghrr (*https://oreil.ly/eKBdi*), but we still think it's better to not spend too much time on or give too much weight to stars.

11 For example, we might ask you to star our example repo (*https://oreil.ly/u6S0H*), and by doing this, we (hopefully) increase the number of stars without actually needing to increase our quality.

Figure 8-2. Someone selling GitHub stars

Code and Best Practices

Software testing is second nature to many software engineers, but sometimes projects are created hastily without tests. If a project does not have tests, and tests that are mostly passing, then it's much harder to have confidence in how the project will behave. Even in the most professional of projects, corners sometimes get cut when it comes to testing, and adding more tests to a project can be a great way to ensure that it continues to function in the ways you need it to. A good question is if the tests cover the parts that are important to you. If a project does have relevant tests, the next natural question is if they are being used. If it's too difficult to run tests, human nature often takes over, and the tests may not be run. So a good step is to see if you can run the tests in the project.

Test coverage numbers can be especially informative, but unfortunately, for projects built on top of systems like Dask,[12] getting accurate test coverage information is a challenge. Instead, a more qualitative approach is often needed here. In single-machine systems, test coverage can be an excellent automatically computed quantitative metric.

We believe that most good libraries will have some form of continuous integration (CI) or automated testing, including proposed changes (or when a pull request is created). You can check if a GitHub project has continuous integration by looking at the pull-requests tab. CI can be very helpful for reducing bugs overall, especially regressions.[13] Historically, use of CI was somewhat a matter of project preference, but with the creation of free tools, including GitHub actions, many multi-person software projects now have some form of CI. This is a common software engineering practice, and we consider it essential for libraries that we depend on.

Static typing is frequently considered a programming best practice, though there are some detractors. While the arguments for and against static types inside data pipelines are complex, we believe *some* typing at the library level is something one should expect.

Conclusion

When building data (or other) applications on Dask, you will likely need many different tools from the ecosystem. The ecosystem evolves at different rates, with some parts requiring more investment by you before you can use them effectively. Choosing the right tools, and transitively the right people, is key to whether your project will succeed and, in our experience, to how enjoyable your work will be. It's important to remember that these decisions are not set in stone, but changing a library tends to get harder the longer you've been using it in your project. In this chapter, you've learned how to evaluate the different components of the ecosystem for project maturity. You can use this knowledge to decide when to use a library versus writing the functionality you need yourself.

---

12 This is because most of the Python tools that check code coverage assume that there is only one Python VM they need to attach to and see what parts of code are executed. However, in a distributed system, this is no longer the case, and many of these automated tools do not work.

13 Where something that used to work stops working in a newer release.

## CHAPTER 9

Migrating Existing Analytic Engineering

Many users will already have analytic work that is currently deployed and that they want to migrate over to Dask. This chapter will discuss the considerations, challenges, and experiences of users making the switch. The main migration pathway explored in the chapter is moving an existing big data engineering job from another distributed framework, such as Spark, into Dask.

Why Dask?

Here are some reasons to consider migrating to Dask from an existing job that is implemented in pandas, or distributed libraries like PySpark:

Python and PyData stack
> Many data scientists and developers prefer using a Python-native stack, where they don't have to switch between languages or styles.

Richer ML integrations with Dask APIs
> Futures, delayed, and ML integrations require less glue code from the developer to maintain, and there are performance improvements from the more flexible task graph management Dask offers.

Fine-grained task management
> Dask's task graph is generated and maintained in real time during runtime, and users can access the task dictionary synchronously.

Debugging overhead
> Some developer teams prefer the debugging experience in Python, as opposed to mixed Python and Java/Scala stacktrace.

Development overhead
> The development step in Dask can be done locally with ease with the developer's laptop, as opposed to needing to connect to a powerful cloud machine in order to experiment.

Management UX
> Dask visualization tools tend to be more visually pleasing and intuitive to reason, with native graphviz rendering for task graphs.

These are not all of the benefits, but if any of them speak to you, it's probably worth investing the time to consider moving the workload to Dask. There are always trade-offs involved, so the next section will look at some of the limitations, followed by a road map to give you an idea of the scale of work involved in moving to Dask.

Limitations of Dask

Dask is relatively new, and the use of Python data stack to perform large-scale extract, transform, load operations is also fairly new. There are limitations to Dask, which mainly arise from the fact that PyData stack has traditionally not been used to perform large-scale data workloads. At the time of writing, there are some limits to the system. However, they are being addressed by developers, and a lot of these deficiencies will be filled in. Some of the fine-grained considerations you should have are as follows:

Parquet scale limits
> If Parquet data exceeds 10 TB in scale, there are issues at the fastparquet and PyArrow level that slow Dask down, and metadata management overhead can be overwhelming.
>
> ETL workloads with Parquet files at 10 TB in scale and beyond, and that include a mutation, such as append and update, run into consistency issues.

Weak data lake integrations
> PyData stack has not engaged much in the big data world traditionally, and the integrations on data lake management, such as Apache Iceberg, are missing.

High-level query optimization
> Users of Spark would be familiar with the Catalyst optimizer that pushes down predicates for optimizing the physical work on the executors. This optimization layer is missing in Dask at the moment. Spark in its early years also did not have the Catalyst engine written yet, and there is work in progress to build this out for Dask.

Any list of limitations for a rapidly developing project like Dask may be out of date by the time you read it, so if any of these are blockers for your migration, make sure to check Dask's status tracker.

Migration Road Map

While no engineering work is linear in process, it's always a good idea to have a road map in mind. We've laid out an example of migration steps as a non-exhaustive list of items a team might want to think through when planning its move:

- What kind of machines and containerization framework will we want to deploy Dask on, and what are their pros and cons?
- Do we have tests to ensure our migration correctness and our desired goals?
- What type of data is Dask able to ingest, and at what scale, and how does that differ from other platforms?
- What is the computation framework of Dask, and how do we think in Dask and Pythonic ways to achieve the task?
- How would we monitor and troubleshoot the code at runtime?

We'll start by looking at the types of clusters, which goes with the deployment framework, as it is often one of the issues requiring collaboration with other teams or organizations.

Types of Clusters

If you are considering moving your analytic engineering job, you probably have a system that's provisioned to you by your organization. Dask is supported in many commonly used deployment and development environments, with some allowing more flexibility in scaling, dependency management, and support of heterogeneous worker types. We have used Dask on academic environments, on commodity cloud, and directly over VMs/containers; we've detailed the pros and cons, and some well-used and supported environments, in Appendix A.

Example 9-1 shows an example of a YARN deployment. More examples and in-depth discussion can be found in Chapter 12.

Example 9-1. Deploying Dask on YARN with Dask-Yarn and skein

```
from dask_yarn import YarnCluster
from dask.distributed import Client

# Create a cluster where each worker has two cores and 8 GiB of memory
cluster = YarnCluster(
    environment='your_environment.tar.gz',
    worker_vcores=2,
    worker_memory="4GiB")

# Scale out to num_workers such workers
cluster.scale(num_workers)
```

```
# Connect to the cluster
client = Client(cluster)
```

If your organization has multiple clusters that are supported, choosing one where you can self-serve dependency management, like Kubernetes, is beneficial.

For high-performance computing deployments using job queuing systems such as PBS, Slurm, MOAB, SGE, LSF, and HTCondor, you should use Dask-jobqueue, as shown in Example 9-2.

Example 9-2. Deploying Dask using jobqueue over Slurm

```
from dask_jobqueue import SLURMCluster
from dask.distributed import Client

cluster = SLURMCluster(
    queue='regular',
    account="slurm_caccount",
    cores=24,
    memory="500 GB"
)
cluster.scale(jobs=SLURM_JOB_COUNT)  # Ask for N jobs from Slurm

client = Client(cluster)

# Auto-scale between 10 and 100 jobs
cluster.adapt(minimum_jobs=10, maximum_jobs=100)
cluster.adapt(maximum_memory="10 TB")  # Or use core/memory limits
```

You likely have a shared filesystem already set up by your organization's admin. Enterprise users might be used to already robustly provisioned distributed data sources, running on HDFS or blob storage like S3, which Dask works with seamlessly (see Example 9-3). Dask also integrates well with networked filesystems.

Example 9-3. Reading and writing to blob storage using MinIO

```
import s3fs
import pyarrow as pa
import pyarrow.parquet as pq

minio_storage_options = {
    "key": MINIO_KEY,
    "secret": MINIO_SECRET,
    "client_kwargs": {
        "endpoint_url": "http://ENDPOINT_URL",
        "region_name": 'us-east-1'
    },
    "config_kwargs": {"s3": {"signature_version": 's3v4'}},
```

```
}

df.to_parquet(f's3://s3_destination/{filename}',
              compression="gzip",
              storage_options=minio_storage_options,
              engine="fastparquet")


df = dd.read_parquet(
    f's3://s3_source/',
    storage_options=minio_storage_options,
    engine="pyarrow"
)
```

We found that one of the surprisingly useful use cases is connecting directly to network storage such as NFS or FTP. When working on an academic dataset that's large and clunky to work with (like a neuroimaging dataset that's directly hosted by another organization), we could connect directly to the source filesystem. When using Dask this way, you should test out and consider network timeout allowances. Also note that, as of this writing, Dask does not have a connector to data lakes such as Iceberg.

Development: Considerations

Translating an existing logic to Dask is a fairly intuitive process. The following sections present some considerations if you're coming from libraries such as R, pandas, and Spark, and how Dask might differ from them. Some of these differences result from moving from a different low-level implementation, such as Java, and others result from moving from single-machine code to a scaled implementation, as when you're coming from pandas.

DataFrame performance

If you have a job that you are already running on a different platform, it's likely you are already using columnar storage format, like Parquet, and reading at runtime. The data type mapping from Parquet to Python is inherently imprecise. It's a good idea to check data types when reading in any data at runtime, and the same applies to DataFrame. If type inference fails, a column would default to object. Once you inspect and determine the type inference is imprecise, specifying data types can speed up your job a lot. Additionally, it's always a good idea to check strings, floating point numbers, datetime, and arrays. If type errors arise, keeping in mind the upstream data sources and their data type is a good start. For example, if the Parquet is generated from protocol buffers, depending on what encode and decode engine was used, there are differences in null checks, float, doubles, and mixed precision types that are introduced in that stack.

When reading a large file from cloud storage into DataFrame, it may be useful to select columns ahead of time at the DataFrame read stage. Users from other platforms like Spark would be familiar with predicate push-down, where even if you don't quite specify the columns desired, the platform would optimize and read only the required column for computation. Dask doesn't quite provide that optimization yet.

Setting smart indices early in the transformation of your DataFrame, prior to a complex query, can speed things up. Be aware that multi-indexing is not supported by Dask yet. A common workaround for a multi-indexed DataFrame from other platforms is mapping as a single concatenated column. For example, a simple work-around when coming from a non-Dask columnar dataset, like pandas pd.MultiIndex that has two columns as its index—say, col1 and col2—would be to introduce a new column in Dask DataFrame col1_col2 as Dask.

During the transform stage, calling .compute() coalesces a large distributed Dask DataFrame to a single partition that should fit in RAM. If it does not, you may encounter problems. On the other hand, if you have filtered an input data of size 100 GB down to 10 GB (say your RAM is 15 GB), it is probably a good idea to reduce the parallelism after the filter operation by invoking .compute(). You can check your DataFrame's memory usage by invoking df.memory_usage(deep=True).sum() to determine if this is the right call. Doing this can be particularly useful if, after the filter operation, you have a complex and expensive shuffle operation, such as .join() with a new larger dataset.

 Dask DataFrame is not value-mutable in the way that pandas Data-Frame users might be familiar with. Since in-memory modification of a particular value is not possible, the only way to change a value would be a map operation over the whole column of the entire DataFrame. If an in-memory value change is something you have to do often, it is better to use an external database.

Porting SQL to Dask

Dask does not natively offer a SQL engine, although it does natively offer options to read from a SQL database. There are a number of different libraries you can use to interact with an existing SQL database, and to treat Dask DataFrame as a SQL table and run SQL queries directly (see Example 9-4). Some allow you to even build and serve ML models directly using SQL ML syntax similar to that of Google's BigQuery ML. In Examples 11-14 and 11-15, we will show the use of Dask's native read_sql() function and running SQL ML using Dask-SQL.

Example 9-4. Reading from a Postgres database

```
df = dd.read_sql_table('accounts', 'sqlite:///path/to/your.db',
                       npartitions=10, index_col='id')
```

FugueSQL provides SQL compatibility to PyData stack, including Dask. The project is in its infancy but seems promising. The main advantage of FugueSQL is that the code is portable between pandas, Dask, and Spark, giving a lot more interoperability. FugueSQL can run its SQL queries using `DaskExecutionEngine`, or you can run FugueSQL queries over a Dask DataFrame you already are using. Alternatively, you can run a quick SQL query on Dask DataFrame on your notebook as well. Example 9-5 shows an example of using FugueSQL in a notebook. The downside of FugueSQL is that it requires the ANTLR library, which in turn requires a Java runtime.

Example 9-5. Running SQL over Dask DataFrame with FugueSQL

```
from fugue_notebook import setup
setup (is_lab=True)
ur = ('https://d37ci6vzurychx.cloudfront.net/trip-data/'
      'yellow_tripdata_2018-01.parquet')
df = dd.read_parquet(url)

%%fsql dask
tempdf = SELECT VendorID, AVG (total_amount) AS average_fare FROM df
GROUP BY VendorID

SELECT *
FROM tempdf
ORDER BY average fare DESC
LIMIT 5
PRINT
```

	VendorID	average_fare
0	1	15.127384
1	2	15.775723

```
schema: VendorID:long, average_fare:double
```

An alternate method is to use the Dask-SQL library. This package uses Apache Calcite to provide the SQL parsing frontend and is used to query Dask DataFrames. With that library, you can pass most of the SQL-based operations to the Dask-SQL context, and it will be handled. The engine handles standard SQL inputs like SELECT, CREATE TABLE, but also ML model creation, with the CREATE MODEL syntax.

Deployment Monitoring

Like many other distributed libraries, Dask provides logs, and you can configure Dask logs to be sent to a storage system. The method will vary by the deployment environment, and whether Jupyter is involved.

The Dask client exposes the `get_worker_logs()` and `get_scheduler_logs()` methods, which can be accessed at runtime if desired. Additionally, similar to other distributed system logging, you can log events by topic, making them easily accessible by event types.

Example 9-6 is a toy example of adding a custom log event to the client.

Example 9-6. Basic logging by topic

```
from dask.distributed import Client

client = Client()
client.log_event(topic="custom_events", msg="hello world")
client.get_events("custom_events")
```

Example 9-7 builds on the previous example, but swaps in the execution context to a distributed cluster setup, for potentially more complex, custom structured events. The Dask client listens and accumulates these events, and we can inspect them. We start with a Dask DataFrame and then run some compute-heavy task. This example uses a `softmax` function, which is a common computation in many ML uses. A common ML dilemma is whether to use a more complex activation or loss function for accuracy, sacrificing performance (thereby running fewer training epochs but gaining a more stable gradient), or vice versa. To figure that out, we insert a code to log custom structured events to time the compute overhead of that specific function.

Example 9-7. Structured logging on workers

```
from dask.distributed import Client, LocalCluster

client = Client(cluster)  # Connect to distributed cluster and override default

d = {'x': [3.0, 1.0, 0.2], 'y': [2.0, 0.5, 0.1], 'z': [1.0, 0.2, 0.4]}
scores_df = dd.from_pandas(pd.DataFrame(data=d), npartitions=1)


def compute_softmax(partition, axis=0):
    """ computes the softmax of the logits
    :param logits: the vector to compute the softmax over
    :param axis: the axis we are summing over
    :return: the softmax of the vector
    """
    if partition.empty:
```

```
    return
import timeit
x = partition[['x', 'y', 'z']].values.tolist()
start = timeit.default_timer()
axis = 0
e = np.exp(x - np.max(x))
ret = e / np.sum(e, axis=axis)
stop = timeit.default_timer()
partition.log_event("softmax", {"start": start, "x": x, "stop": stop})
dask.distributed.get_worker().log_event(
    "softmax", {"start": start, "input": x, "stop": stop})
return ret


scores_df.apply(compute_softmax, axis=1, meta=object).compute()
client.get_events("softmax")
```

Conclusion

In this chapter you have reviewed the large questions and considerations of migrating existing analytic engineering work. You've also learned some of the feature differences of Dask compared to Spark, R, and pandas. Some features are not yet implemented by Dask, some are more robustly implemented by Dask, and others are inherent translational differences when moving a computation from a single machine to a distributed cluster. Since large-scale data engineering tends to use similar terms and names across many libraries, it's often easy to overlook minute differences that lead to larger performance or correctness issues. Keeping them in mind will help you as you take your first journeys in Dask.

## CHAPTER 10

Dask with GPUs and Other Special Resources

Sometimes the answer to our scaling problem isn't throwing more computers at it; it's throwing different types of resources at it. One example of this might be ten thousand monkeys trying to reproduce the works of Shakespeare, versus one Shakespeare.[1] While performance varies, some benchmarks have shown up to an 85% improvement in model training times (*https://oreil.ly/Iw3Sv*) when using GPUs over CPUs. Continuing its modular tradition, the GPU logic of Dask is found in the libraries and ecosystem surrounding it. The libraries can either run on a collection of GPU workers or parallelize work over different GPUs on one host.

Most work we do on the computer is done on the CPU. GPUs were created for displaying video but involve doing large amounts of vectorized floating point (e.g., non-integer) operations. With vectorized operations, the same operation is applied in parallel on large sets of data, like a map. Tensor Processing Units (TPUs) are similar to GPUs, except without also being used for graphics.

For our purposes, in Dask, we can think of GPUs and TPUs as specializing in offloading large vectorized computations, but there are many other kinds of accelerators. While much of this chapter is focused on GPUs, the same general techniques, albeit with different libraries, generally apply to other accelerators. Other kinds of specialized resources include NVMe drives, faster (or larger) RAM, TCP/IP offload, Just-a-Bunch-of-Disks expansion ports, and Intel's OPTAIN memory. Special resources/accelerators can improve everything from network latency to writing large files to disk. What all these share is that Dask has no built-in understanding of these

---

1 Assuming Shakespeare were still alive, which he is not.

resources, and it's up to you to provide that information to the Dask scheduler and also take advantage of it.

This chapter will look at the current state of accelerated analytics in Python and how to use these tools together with Dask. You will learn what kinds of problems are well suited to GPU acceleration, a bit about other kinds of accelerators, and how to apply this knowledge to your problems.

 Cloud accounts and machines with access to GPUs are especially of interest to less-than-savory folks on the internet due to the relative ease of mining cryptocurrency. If you are used to working with only public data and lax security controls, take this as an opportunity to review your security process and restrict runtime access to only those who need it. Or be prepared for a really large cloud bill.

Transparent Versus Non-transparent Accelerators

Accelerators largely break down into two categories: transparent (no code or change required) and non-transparent optimizers. Whether an accelerator is transparent or not largely depends on whether someone below us in the stack has made it transparent to us.

TCP/IP offloading is generally transparent at the user space level, which means the operating system takes care of it for us. NVMe drives are also generally transparent, generally appearing the same as spinning disks, except faster. It is still important to make Dask aware of transparent optimizers; for example, a disk-intensive workload should be scheduled on the machines with faster disks.

The non-transparent accelerators include GPUs, Optane, QAT, and many more. Using these requires changing our code to be able to take advantage of them. Sometimes this can be as simple as swapping in a different library, but not always. Many non-transparent accelerators require either copying our data or special formatting to be able to operate. This means that if an operation is relatively fast, moving to an optimizer could make it slower.

Understanding Whether GPUs or TPUs Can Help

Not every problem is a good fit for GPU acceleration. GPUs are especially good at performing the same calculation on a large number of data points at the same time. If a problem is well suited to vectorized computation, then there is a good chance that GPUs may be well suited to it.

Some common problems that benefit from GPU acceleration include:

- Machine learning
- Linear algebra
- Physics simulations
- Graphics (no surprise here)

GPUs are not well suited to branch-heavy non-vectorized workflows, or workflows where the cost of copying the data is similar to or higher than the cost of the computation.

Making Dask Resource-Aware

If you have decided that your problem is well suited to a specialized resource, the next step is to make the scheduler aware of which machines and processes have the resource (*https://oreil.ly/EHFTr*). You can do this by adding either an environment variable or a command-line flag to the worker launch (e.g., `--resources "GPU=2"` or `DASK_DISTRIBUTED__WORKER__RESOURCES__GPU=2`).

For NVIDIA users, the `dask-cuda` package can launch one worker per GPU, pinning the GPU and thread together for performance. For example, on our Kubernetes cluster with GPU resources, we configure the workers to use the `dask-cuda-worker` launcher, as shown in Example 10-1.

Example 10-1. Using the `dask-cuda-worker` package in the Dask Kubernetes template

```
worker_template = make_pod_spec(image='holdenk/dask:latest',
                                memory_limit='8G', memory_request='8G',
                                cpu_limit=1, cpu_request=1)
worker_template.spec.containers[0].resources.limits["gpu"] = 1
worker_template.spec.containers[0].resources.requests["gpu"] = 1
worker_template.spec.containers[0].args[0] = "dask-cuda-worker --resources 'GPU=1'"
worker_template.spec.containers[0].env.append("NVIDIA_VISIBLE_DEVICES=ALL")
# Or append --resources "GPU=2"
```

Here you see we still add the `--resources` flag so that in a mixed environment we can select just the GPU workers.

If you're using Dask to schedule work on multiple GPUs on a single computer (e.g., using Dask local mode with CUDA), the same `dask-cuda` package provides a `LocalCUDACluster`. As with `dask-cuda-worker`, you still need to add the resource tag manually, as shown in Example 10-2, but `LocalCUDACluster` launches the correct workers and pins them to threads.

Example 10-2. `LocalCUDACluster` with resource tagging

```
from dask_cuda import LocalCUDACluster
from dask.distributed import Client
#NOTE: The resources= flag is important; by default the
# LocalCUDACluster *does not* label any resources, which can make
# porting your code to a cluster where some workers have GPUs and
# some don't painful.
cluster = LocalCUDACluster(resources={"GPU": 1})
client = Client(cluster)
```

 For homogeneous clusters it may seem tempting to avoid labeling these resources, but unless you will always have a 1:1 mapping of worker process/thread to the accelerator (or the accelerator can be used by all workers at the same time), it is still beneficial to label these resources. This is important for non-shareable (or difficult-to-share) resources like GPUs/TPUs since Dask might schedule two tasks trying to access the GPU. But for shareable resources like NVMe drives, or TCP/IP offloading, if it's present on every node in the cluster and will always be, you can probably skip it.

It's important to note that Dask does not manage custom resources (including GPUs). If another process uses all of the GPU cores without asking Dask, there is no protection for this. In some ways, this is reminiscent of early computing, where we had "cooperative" multi-tasking; we depend on our neighbors being well behaved.

 Dask depends on well-behaved Python code, which does not use resources it has not asked for and releases the resources when finished. This most commonly happens with memory leaks (both accelerated and not), often with specialized libraries like CUDA that allocate memory outside of Python. These libraries often have special steps you need to call when you are done with the task you've asked to make the resources available for others.

Installing the Libraries

Now that Dask is aware of the special resources on your cluster, it's time to make sure that your code can take advantage of them. Often, but not always, these accelerators will require some kind of special library to be installed, which may involve long compile times. When possible, installing the acceleration libraries from conda and pre-installing on the workers (in the container or on the host) can help minimize this overhead.

For Kubernetes (or other Docker container users), you can do this by making a custom container with the accelerator libraries pre-installed, as seen in Example 10-3.

Example 10-3. Pre-installing cuDF

```
# Use the Dask base image; for arm64, though, we have to use custom built
# FROM ghcr.io/dask/dask
FROM holdenk/dask:latest

# arm64 channel
RUN conda config --add channels rpi
# Numba and conda-forge channels
RUN conda config --add channels numba
RUN conda config --add channels conda-forge
# Some CUDA-specific stuff
RUN conda config --add channels rapidsai
# Accelerator libraries often involve a lot of native code, so it's
# faster to install with conda
RUN conda install numba -y
# GPU support (NV)
RUN conda install cudatoolkit -y
# GPU support (AMD)
RUN conda install roctools -y || echo "No roc tools on $(uname -a)"
# A lot of GPU acceleration libraries are in the rapidsai channel
# These are not installable with pip
RUN conda install cudf -y
```

Then, to build this, we run the script shown in Example 10-4.

Example 10-4. Building custom Dask Docker containers

```
#/bin/bash
set -ex

docker buildx build -t holdenk/dask-extended  --platform \
  linux/arm64,linux/amd64 --push . -f Dockerfile
docker buildx build -t holdenk/dask-extended-notebook  --platform \
  linux/arm64,linux/amd64 --push . -f NotebookDockerfile
```

Using Custom Resources Inside Your Dask Tasks

It is important that you make sure your tasks that need accelerators run on worker processes with the accelerator available. You can ask for special resources when scheduling tasks with Dask, either explicitly in `client.submit`, as seen in Example 10-5, or by adding an annotation to your existing code, as seen in Example 10-6.

Example 10-5. Submitting a task asking for a GPU

```
future = client.submit(how_many_gpus, 1, resources={'GPU': 1})
```

Example 10-6. Annotating a group of operations as needing a GPU

```
with dask.annotate(resources={'GPU': 1}):
    future = client.submit(how_many_gpus, 1)
```

If you move from a cluster with GPU resources to a cluster without, this code will hang indefinitely. The CPU Fallback design pattern covered later can mitigate this.

Decorators (Including Numba)

Numba is a popular high-performance JIT compilation library for Python, which also has support for various accelerators. Most JIT code, as well as many decorator functions, is generally not directly serializable, so attempting to directly Numba it with dask.submit, as seen in Example 10-7, does not work. Instead, the correct way is to wrap the function, as shown in Example 10-8.

Example 10-7. Decorator difficulty

```
# Works in local mode, but not distributed
@dask.delayed
@guvectorize(['void(float64[:], intp[:], float64[:])'],
             '(n),()->(n)')
def delayed_move_mean(a, window_arr, out):
    window_width = window_arr[0]
    asum = 0.0
    count = 0
    for i in range(window_width):
        asum += a[i]
        count += 1
        out[i] = asum / count
    for i in range(window_width, len(a)):
        asum += a[i] - a[i - window_width]
        out[i] = asum / count


arr = np.arange(20, dtype=np.float64).reshape(2, 10)
print(arr)
print(dask.compute(delayed_move_mean(arr, 3)))
```

Example 10-8. Decorator hack

```
@guvectorize(['void(float64[:], intp[:], float64[:])'],
             '(n),()->(n)')
def move_mean(a, window_arr, out):
    window_width = window_arr[0]
    asum = 0.0
    count = 0
    for i in range(window_width):
        asum += a[i]
```

```
        count += 1
        out[i] = asum / count
    for i in range(window_width, len(a)):
        asum += a[i] - a[i - window_width]
        out[i] = asum / count


arr = np.arange(20, dtype=np.float64).reshape(2, 10)
print(arr)
print(move_mean(arr, 3))


def wrapped_move_mean(*args):
    return move_mean(*args)


a = dask.delayed(wrapped_move_mean)(arr, 3)
```

 Example 10-7 will work in local mode—but not when you go to scale.

GPUs

Like most tasks in Python, there are many different libraries for working with GPUs. Many of these libraries support NVIDIA's Compute Unified Device Architecture (CUDA) with experimental support for AMD's new open HIP/Radeon Open Compute module (ROCm) interfaces. NVIDIA and CUDA were the first on the scene and have a much larger adoption than AMD's Radeon Open Compute module—so much so that ROCm has a large focus on supporting ports of CUDA software to the ROCm platform.

We won't dive deep into the world of Python GPU libraries, but you may want to check out Numba for GPUs (*https://oreil.ly/i-FVO*), TensorFlow GPU support (*https://oreil.ly/vChSG*), and PyTorch's GPU support (*https://oreil.ly/sdLjo*).

Most of the libraries that have some form of GPU support require compiling large amounts of non-Python code. As such, it's often best to install these libraries with conda, which frequently has more complete binary packaging, allowing you to skip the compile step.

GPU Acceleration Built on Top of Dask

The three main CUDA libraries extending Dask are cuDF (previously called dask-cudf), BlazingSQL, and cuML.[2] Currently these libraries are focused on NVIDIA GPUs.

Dask does not currently have any libraries powering integrations with OpenCL or HIP. This does not preclude you in any way from using GPUs with libraries that support them, like TensorFlow, as previously illustrated.

cuDF

cuDF (*https://oreil.ly/BZ9x2*) is a GPU-accelerated version of Dask's DataFrame library. Some benchmarking shows performance speed-ups of 7x~50x (*https://oreil.ly/unpvl*). Not all DataFrame operations will have this same speed-up. For example, if you are operating row-by-row instead of in vectorized type operations, you may experience slower performance when using cuDF over Dask's DataFrame library. cuDF supports most of the common data types you are likely to use, but not all.

Under the hood, cuDF frequently delegates work to the cuPY library, but since it is created by NVIDIA employees and their focus is on supporting NVIDIA hardware, cuDF does not have direct support for ROCm.

BlazingSQL

BlazingSQL uses GPU acceleration to provide super-fast SQL queries. BlazingSQL operates on top of cuDF.

While BlazingSQL is a wonderful tool, much of its documentation is broken. For example, at the time of this writing, none of the examples linked in the main README resolve correctly, and the documentation site is entirely offline.

---

2 BlazingSQL may be at the end of its life; there has not been a commit for an extended period of time, and the website is just a hard hat, like those 1990s GeoCities websites.

---

cuStreamz

Another GPU-accelerated library for streaming on GPUs is cuStreamz, which is basically a combination of Dask streaming and cuDF; we cover it more in Appendix D.

Freeing Accelerator Resources

Allocating memory on GPUs tends to be slow, so many libraries hold on to these resources. In most situations, if the Python VM exits, the resources will be cleared up. An option of last resort is to bounce all of the workers using `client.restart`. When possible, you will be best served by manually managing resources—which is library-dependent. For example, cuPY users can free the blocks once used by calling `free_all_blocks()`, as per the memory management documentation (*https://oreil.ly/hpxkg*).

Design Patterns: CPU Fallback

CPU Fallback refers to attempting to use an accelerator, like GPU or TPU, and falling back to the regular CPU code path if the accelerator is unavailable. In most cases, this is a good design pattern to follow, as accelerators (like GPUs) can be expensive and may not always be available. However, in some cases, the difference between CPU and GPU performance is so large that falling back to the CPU is unlikely to be able to succeed in a practical amount of time; this occurs most often with deep learning algorithms.

Object-oriented programming and duck-typing are somewhat well suited to this design pattern, since, provided that two classes implement the same parts of the interface you are using, you can swap them around. However, much like swapping in Dask DataFrames for pandas DataFrames, it is imperfect, especially when it comes to performance.

 In a better world, we could submit a task requesting GPU resources, and if that does not get scheduled, we could switch back to CPU-only resources. Unfortunately, Dask's resources scheduling is closer to "best effort,"[3] so we may be scheduled on nodes without the resources we request.

---

3 This is not as documented (*https://oreil.ly/p1Ldf*), and so may change in the future.

Conclusion

Specialized accelerators, like GPUs, can make large differences in your workflows. Picking the right accelerator for your workflow is important, and some workflows are not well suited to acceleration. Dask does not automate the usage of any accelerators, but there are various libraries that you can use for GPU computation. Many of these libraries were not created with the idea of shared computation in mind, so it's important to be on the lookout for accidental resource leaks, especially since GPU resources tend to be more expensive.

## CHAPTER 11

Machine Learning with Dask

Now that you know Dask's many different data types, computation patterns, deployment options, and libraries, we are ready to tackle machine learning. You will quickly find that ML with Dask is quite intuitive to use, as it runs on the same Python environment as the many other popular ML libraries. Much of the heavy work is done by Dask's built-in data types and Dask's distributed schedulers, making writing code an enjoyable experience for the user.[1]

This chapter will primarily use the Dask-ML library, a robustly supported ML library from the Dask open source project, but we will also highlight other libraries, such as XGBoost and scikit-learn. The Dask-ML library is designed to run both in clusters and locally.[2] Dask-ML provides familiar interfaces by extending many common ML libraries. ML is different from many of the tasks discussed so far, as it requires the framework (here Dask-ML) to coordinate work more closely. In this chapter we'll show some of the ways you can use it in your own programs, and we'll also offer tips.

Since ML is such a wide and varied discipline, we are able to cover only some of the situations where Dask-ML is useful. This chapter will discuss some of the common work patterns, such as exploratory data analysis, random split, featurization, regression, and deep learning inferences, from a practitioner's perspective on ramping up on Dask. If you don't see your particular library or use case represented, it may still be possible to accelerate with Dask, and you should look at Dask-ML's API guide (*https://oreil.ly/eJGHU*). However, ML is not Dask's primary focus, so you may find that you need to use other tools, like Ray.

---

1 For those inclined to think that writing data engineering code is "fun."

2 This is especially important for non-batch inference, where being able to use the same code can be of great benefit.

Parallelizing ML

Many ML workloads face scaling challenges in two dimensions: model size and data size. Training models with large features or components, like many deep learning models, often become compute-bound, where training, predicting, and evaluating the model becomes slow and harder to manage. On the other hand, many ML models, even seemingly simple ones like regression, often get stretched to their limits with large volumes of training datasets that don't fit into one machine, getting memory-bound in their scaling challenges.

On memory-bound workloads, Dask's high-level collections that we have covered (such as Dask array, DataFrame, and bag) combine with Dask-ML libraries to offer native scaling. For compute-bound workloads, Dask parallelizes training through integrations such as Dask-ML and Dask-joblib. In the case of scikit-learn, Dask can manage cluster-wide work allocation, using Dask-joblib. You might notice each workflow requires a different library; this is because each ML tool uses its own method of parallelization that Dask extends.

You can use Dask in conjunction with many popular machine learning libraries, including scikit-learn and XGBoost. You may already be familiar with single-machine parallelism inside your favorite ML library. Dask takes these single-machine frame-works, like Dask-joblib, and extends them to machines connected over the network.

When to Use Dask-ML

Dask excels in parallel tasks with limited distributed mutable state (like large model weights). Dask is commonly used for inference/predictions on ML models, which is simpler than training. Training models, on the other hand, often require more inter-worker communication in the form of model weight updates and repeated loops, with sometimes variable amounts of computation per training cycle. You can use Dask for both of these use cases, but adoption and tooling for training is not as widespread.

Dask's integration with common data preparation tools—including pandas, NumPy, PyTorch, and TensorFlow—makes it easier to build inference pipelines. In JVM-based tools, like Spark, working with those libraries comes at a higher overhead.

Another great use case for Dask is feature engineering and plotting large datasets before training. Dask's pre-processing functions often use the same signatures, and function the same way as scikit-learn, while distributing the work across machines. Similarly with plotting and visualization, Dask is able to generate a beautiful plot of a large dataset beyond the usual limits of matplotlib/seaborn.

For more involved ML and deep learning work, some users opt to generate PyTorch or TensorFlow models separately and then use the models generated for inference workloads using Dask. This keeps the workload on the Dask side embarrassingly parallel. Alternatively, some users opt to write the training data as a Dask DataFrame using the delayed pattern, which is fed into Keras or Torch. Be warned that there is a medium level of effort to do so.

As discussed in previous chapters, the Dask project is still in the early phase of its life, and some of these libraries are still a work in progress and come with disclaimers. We took extra caution to validate most of the numerical methods used in the Dask-ML library to make sure the logic and mathematics are sound and work as expected. However, some dependent libraries come with warnings that it's not yet ready for prime time, especially as it relates to GPU-aware workloads and massively distributed workloads. We expect these to get sorted out as the community grows and users contribute their feedback.

Getting Started with Dask-ML and XGBoost

Dask-ML is the officially supported ML library for Dask. Here, we will walk through the functionalities provided in the Dask-ML API; how it connects Dask, pandas, and scikit-learn into its functions; and some differences between Dask and its scikit-learn equivalents. Additionally, we will walk through a few XGBoost gradient boost integrations. We will primarily use the New York City yellow taxicab data we used previously to walk through examples. You can access the dataset directly from the New York City website (*https://oreil.ly/lbU5V*).

Feature Engineering

As with any good data science workflow, we start with clean-up, applying scalers, and transforms. Dask-ML has drop-in replacements for most of the pre-processing API from scikit-learn, including StandardScaler, PolynomialFeatures, MinMax Scaler, etc.

You can pass multiple columns to the transformers, and each will be normalized, resulting in a delayed Dask DataFrame that you should call compute on.

In Example 11-1, we scale trip distances, which are in miles, and total amount, which is in dollars, to their own scaled variables. This is a continuation of the exploratory data analysis we did in Chapter 4.

Example 11-1. Dask DataFrame pre-processing with StandardScaler

```
from dask_ml.preprocessing import StandardScaler
import dask.array as da
import numpy as np

df = dd.read_parquet(url)
```

```
trip_dist_df = df[["trip_distance", "total_amount"]]
scaler = StandardScaler()

scaler.fit(trip_dist_df)
trip_dist_df_scaled = scaler.transform(trip_dist_df)
trip_dist_df_scaled.head()
```

For categorical variables, while there is OneHotEncoder in Dask-ML, it's not as efficient or as one-to-one in replacement as its scikit-learn equivalent. At this point we recommend using Categorizer to encode a categorical dtype.[3]

Example 11-2 shows how you would categorize a particular column while preserving the existing DataFrame. We select payment_type, which is encoded originally as an integer but is really a four-category categorical variable. We call Dask-ML's Categorizer, while using pandas's CategoricalDtype to give type hints. While Dask does have type inference (e.g., it can auto-infer the type), it is always better to be explicit in your program.

Example 11-2. Dask DataFrame pre-processing as categorical variable using Dask-ML

```
from dask_ml.preprocessing import Categorizer
from pandas.api.types import CategoricalDtype

payment_type_amt_df = df[["payment_type", "total_amount"]]

cat = Categorizer(categories={"payment_type": CategoricalDtype([1, 2, 3, 4])})
categorized_df = cat.fit_transform(payment_type_amt_df)
categorized_df.dtypes
payment_type_amt_df.head()
```

Alternatively, you can opt to use Dask DataFrame's built-in categorizer. While pandas is permissive with Object and String as categorical data types, Dask will reject these columns unless they are read first as a categorical variable. There are two ways you can do this: declare a column as categorical at reading the data, with dtype={col: categorical}, or convert before invoking get_dummies, by using df .categorize("col1"). The reasoning here is that Dask is lazily evaluated and cannot create a dummy variable out of a column without having a full list of unique values seen. Calling .categorize() is convenient and allows for dynamic handling of additional categories, but keep in mind that it does need to scan the entire column first to get the categories then do another full scan to transform the column. So if you know the categories already and they won't change, you should just invoke DummyEncoder.

---

3 For performance reasons—at the time of writing, Dask's OneHotEncoder calls the get_dummies method from pandas, which is a slower implementation than scikit-learn's OneHotEncoder. Categorizer, on the other hand, uses a Dask DataFrame aggregation method to scan through categories efficiently.

Example 11-3 categorizes multiple columns at once. Nothing is materialized until you call execute, so you can chain many of these pre-processes at once.

Example 11-3. Dask DataFrame pre-processing as categorical variable using the Dask DataFrame built-in

```
train = train.categorize("VendorID")
train = train.categorize("passenger_count")
train = train.categorize("store_and_fwd_flag")

test = test.categorize("VendorID")
test = test.categorize("passenger_count")
test = test.categorize("store_and_fwd_flag")
```

DummyEncoder is the Dask-ML equivalent to scikit-learn's OneHotEncoder, which will turn the variables into uint8, an eight-bit unsigned integer, which is more memory efficient.

Again, there is a Dask DataFrame function that gives you a similar result. Example 11-4 demonstrates this on categorical columns, and Example 11-5 pre-processes datetime. Datetime can be tricky to work with. In this case, Python natively deserializes the datetime. Remember to always check datetime conversion and apply the necessary transforms beforehand.

Example 11-4. Dask DataFrame pre-processing as dummy variable using the Dask DataFrame built-in

```
from dask_ml.preprocessing import DummyEncoder

dummy = DummyEncoder()
dummified_df = dummy.fit_transform(categorized_df)
dummified_df.dtypes
dummified_df.head()
```

Example 11-5. Dask DataFrame pre-processing datetime as dummy variable using the Dask DataFrame built-in

```
train['Hour'] = train['tpep_pickup_datetime'].dt.hour
test['Hour'] = test['tpep_pickup_datetime'].dt.hour

train['dayofweek'] = train['tpep_pickup_datetime'].dt.dayofweek
test['dayofweek'] = test['tpep_pickup_datetime'].dt.dayofweek

train = train.categorize("dayofweek")
test = test.categorize("dayofweek")

dom_train = dd.get_dummies(
    train,
```

```
        columns=['dayofweek'],
        prefix='dom',
        prefix_sep='_')
dom_test = dd.get_dummies(
    test,
    columns=['dayofweek'],
    prefix='dom',
    prefix_sep='_')

hour_train = dd.get_dummies(
    train,
    columns=['dayofweek'],
    prefix='h',
    prefix_sep='_')
hour_test = dd.get_dummies(
    test,
    columns=['dayofweek'],
    prefix='h',
    prefix_sep='_')

dow_train = dd.get_dummies(
    train,
    columns=['dayofweek'],
    prefix='dow',
    prefix_sep='_')
dow_test = dd.get_dummies(
    test,
    columns=['dayofweek'],
    prefix='dow',
    prefix_sep='_')
```

Dask-ML's `train_test_split` method has more flexibility than the Dask DataFrames version. Both are partition-aware, and we using them instead of the scikit-learn equivalent. scikit-learn's `train_test_split` can be called here, but it is not partition-aware and can result in a large data movement between workers, whereas the Dask implementations would split the train-test over each partition, avoiding the shuffle (see Example 11-6).

Example 11-6. Dask DataFrame pseudorandom split

```
from dask_ml.model_selection import train_test_split

X_train, X_test, y_train, y_test = train_test_split(
    df['trip_distance'], df['total_amount'])
```

As a side effect of random splits happening by each partition block, the random behavior is not uniformly guaranteed over the whole of the DataFrame. If you suspect that some partition may have skews, you should compute, redistribute, and then shuffle-split.

Model Selection and Training

Many of scikit-learn's model-selection-related functions, including cross-validation, hyperparameter search, clustering, regression, imputation, and scoring methods, are ported into Dask as a drop-in replacement. There are a few noteworthy improvements that make the functions run more efficiently than a simple parallel computing architecture, by using Dask's task-graph views.

Most regression-based models have been implemented for Dask use and can be used as a replacement for scikit-learn.[4] Many scikit-learn users would be familiar with the task of `.reshape()` for pandas, needing them to convert a pandas DataFrame into a 2D array in order for scikit-learn to work. For some Dask-ML functions you still need to also call `ddf.to_dask_array()` in order to convert a DataFrame to an array before training. Lately, some Dask-ML has been improved to directly work on Dask DataFrames, but not all libraries.

Example 11-7 runs through a straightforward multi-variate linear regression using Dask-ML. Say you want to build a regression model on two predictor columns and one output column. You would apply `.to_array()` to convert the data type to Dask arrays and then pass them into Dask-ML's implementation of `LinearRegression`. Note how we needed to materialize the conversion into arrays, and we gave explicit chunk size. This is because Dask-ML's underlying implementation with linear models is not quite fully able to infer chunk sizes from previous steps. We also purposefully use scikit-learn's scoring library, not Dask-ML. We are noticing implementation issues where Dask-ML doesn't play well with chunk sizes.[5] Thankfully, at this point, this calculation is a reduce step, which works without any Dask-specific logic.[6]

Example 11-7. Linear regression with Dask-ML

```
from dask_ml.linear_model import LinearRegression
from dask_ml.model_selection import train_test_split

regr_df = df[['trip_distance', 'total_amount']].dropna()
regr_X = regr_df[['trip_distance']]
regr_y = regr_df[['total_amount']]

X_train, X_test, y_train, y_test = train_test_split(
    regr_X, regr_y)
```

---

4 Most linear models in Dask-ML use a base implementation of the Generalized Linear Model library that has been implemented for Dask. We have verified the code for mathematical correctness, but the writers of this library have not endorsed the use of their GLM library for prime time yet.

5 Dask-ML version 2023.3.24; some of the generalized linear models used rely on dask-glm 0.1.0.

6 Because it's a simple reduce operation, we don't need to preserve the chunking from previous steps.

```
X_train = X_train.to_dask_array(lengths=[100]).compute()
X_test = X_test.to_dask_array(lengths=[100]).compute()
y_train = y_train.to_dask_array(lengths=[100]).compute()
y_test = y_test.to_dask_array(lengths=[100]).compute()

reg = LinearRegression()
reg.fit(X_train, y_train)
y_pred = reg.predict(X_test)

r2_score(y_test, y_pred)
```

Note that function parameters for models for scikit-learn and Dask-ML are identical, but some are not supported as of now. For example, `LogisticRegression` is available in Dask-ML, but multi-class solver is not supported, meaning that there is no exact equivalent for multi-class solvers implemented in Dask-ML yet. So, if you want to use multinomial loss solver newton-cg or newton-cholesky, it might not work. For most uses of `LogisticRegression`, a default liblinear solver would do the trick. In practice, this limitation would pertain only to more niche and advanced use cases.

For hyperparameter search, Dask-ML has the scikit-learn equivalent of `GridSearchCV` for exhaustive search over parameter values, and `RandomizedSearchCV` for randomly trying hyperparameters from a list. These can be run directly, similar to the scikit-learn variant, if the data and resulting model do not require much scaling.

Cross-validation and hyperparameter tuning often is a costly process even with a smaller dataset, as anyone who has run the scikit-learn cross-validate would attest. Dask users often deal with datasets large enough that use of exhaustive search algorithms is not feasible. As an alternative, Dask-ML implements several additional adaptive algorithms and hyperband-based methods that approach the tuned parameter more quickly with robust mathematical foundation.[7] The authors of the `Hyper bandSearchCV` methods do ask that the use be cited.[8]

When There Is No Dask-ML Equivalent

If there is a function that exists in scikit-learn or other data science libraries but not in Dask-ML, you can write the distributed version of your desired code. After all, Dask-ML can be thought of as a convenience wrapper around scikit-learn.

---

7 Dask-ML's own documentation has more info on adaptive and approximation CV methods implemented and use cases.

8 They note in the documentation that the following paper should be cited if using this method: S. Sievert, T. Augspurger, and M. Rocklin, "Better and Faster Hyperparameter Optimization with Dask," *Proceedings of the 18th Python in Science Conference* (2019), *https://doi.org/10.25080/Majora-7ddc1dd1-011.*

Example 11-8 uses scikit-learn's learning functions `SGDRegressor` and `LinearRegres
sion`, and uses `dask.delayed` to wrap the delayed functionality around the method.
You can do this over any piece of code you may want to parallelize.

Example 11-8. Linear regression with Dask-ML

```
from sklearn.linear_model import LinearRegression as ScikitLinearRegression
from sklearn.linear_model import SGDRegressor as ScikitSGDRegressor

estimators = [ScikitLinearRegression(), ScikitSGDRegressor()]
run_tasks = [dask.delayed(estimator.fit)(X_train, y_train)
            for estimator in estimators]
run_tasks
```

Use with Dask's joblib

Alternatively, you can use scikit-learn along with joblib (see Example 11-9), a package
that can take any Python function as pipelined steps to be computed on a single
machine. Joblib works well with a lot of parallel computations that are not dependent
on each other. In this case, having hundreds of cores on a single machine would be
helpful. While a typical laptop does not have hundreds of cores, using the four or so
that it does have can still be beneficial. With Dask's version of joblib you can use cores
from multiple machines. This can work for ML workloads that are compute-bound
on a single machine.

Example 11-9. Parallelizing computation using joblib

```
from dask.distributed import Client
from joblib import parallel_backend

client = Client('127.0.0.1:8786')

X, y = load_my_data()
net = get_that_net()

gs = GridSearchCV(
    net,
    param_grid={'lr': [0.01, 0.03]},
    scoring='accuracy',
)

XGBClassifier()

with parallel_backend('dask'):
    gs.fit(X, y)
print(gs.cv_results_)
```

XGBoost with Dask

XGBoost is a popular Python gradient boosting library, used for parallel tree boosting. Well-known gradient boosting methods include bootstrap aggregation (bagging). Various gradient boosting methods have been used in high-energy physics data analysis at the Large Hadron Collider, used to train deep neural networks to confirm the discovery of the Higgs boson. Gradient boosting methods are currently used in scientific areas such as geological or climate studies. Given its importance, we found XGBoost on Dask-ML to be a well-implemented library, ready for users.

Dask-ML has built-in support for XGBoost to work with Dask arrays and DataFrames. By using XGBClassifiers within Dask-ML, you will be setting up XGBoost in distributed mode, which works with your Dask cluster. When you do so, XGBoost's master process lives in Dask scheduler, and XGBoost's worker processes will be on Dask's worker processes. The data distribution is handled using Dask DataFrame, split into pandas DataFrame, and is talking between Dask worker and XGBoost worker on the same machine.

XGBoost uses a `DMatrix` (data matrix) as the standard data format it works with. XGBoost has a built-in Dask-compatible `DMatrix`, which takes in Dask array and Dask DataFrame. Once the Dask environment is set up, the use of gradient booster is as you would expect. Specify the learning rate, threads, and objective functions, as usual. Example 11-10 works with a Dask CUDA cluster and runs a standard gradient booster training.

Example 11-10. Gradient-boosted trees with Dask-ML

```
import xgboost as xgb
from dask_cuda import LocalCUDACluster
from dask.distributed import Client

n_workers = 4
cluster = LocalCUDACluster(n_workers)
client = Client(cluster)

dtrain = xgb.dask.DaskDMatrix(client, X_train, y_train)

booster = xgb.dask.train(
    client,
    {"booster": "gbtree", "verbosity": 2, "nthread": 4, "eta": 0.01, gamma=0,
     "max_depth": 5, "tree_method": "auto", "objective": "reg:squarederror"},
    dtrain,
    num_boost_round=4,
    evals=[(dtrain, "train")])
```

In Example 11-11, we run a simple training run and plot feature importance. Note when we define `DMatrix`, we explicitly specify the labels, and the label names are taken from Dask DataFrame into `DMatrix`.

Example 11-11. Dask-ML using the XGBoost library

```
import xgboost as xgb

dtrain = xgb.DMatrix(X_train, label=y_train, feature_names=X_train.columns)
dvalid = xgb.DMatrix(X_test, label=y_test, feature_names=X_test.columns)
watchlist = [(dtrain, 'train'), (dvalid, 'valid')]
xgb_pars = {
    'min_child_weight': 1,
    'eta': 0.5,
    'colsample_bytree': 0.9,
    'max_depth': 6,
    'subsample': 0.9,
    'lambda': 1.,
    'nthread': -1,
    'booster': 'gbtree',
    'silent': 1,
    'eval_metric': 'rmse',
    'objective': 'reg:linear'}
model = xgb.train(xgb_pars, dtrain, 10, watchlist, early_stopping_rounds=2,
                  maximize=False, verbose_eval=1)
print('Modeling RMSLE %.5f' % model.best_score)

xgb.plot_importance(model, max_num_features=28, height=0.7)

pred = model.predict(dtest)
pred = np.exp(pred) - 1
```

Putting the previous examples together, you can now compose a function that can fit a model, provide early stopping arguments, and also define predictions using XGBoost for Dask (see Example 11-12). These would be called in your main client code.

Example 11-12. Gradient-boosted tree training and inference using the Dask XGBoost library

```
import xgboost as xgb
from dask_cuda import LocalCUDACluster
from dask.distributed import Client

n_workers = 4
cluster = LocalCUDACluster(n_workers)
client = Client(cluster)
```

```
def fit_model(client, X, y, X_valid, y_valid,
              early_stopping_rounds=5) -> xgb.Booster:
    Xy_valid = dxgb.DaskDMatrix(client, X_valid, y_valid)
    # train the model
    booster = xgb.dask.train(
        client,
        {"booster": "gbtree", "verbosity": 2, "nthread": 4, "eta": 0.01, gamma=0,
         "max_depth": 5, "tree_method": "gpu_hist", "objective": "reg:squarederror"},
        dtrain,
        num_boost_round=500,
        early_stopping_rounds=early_stopping_rounds,
        evals=[(dtrain, "train")])["booster"]
    return booster


def predict(client, model, X):
    predictions = xgb.predict(client, model, X)
    assert isinstance(predictions, dd.Series)
    return predictions
```

ML Models with Dask-SQL

A much newer addition is another library, Dask-SQL, that provides a convenient wrapper around simple ML model training workloads. Example 11-13 loads the same NYC yellow taxicab data as a Dask DataFrame and then registers the view to Dask-SQL context.

Example 11-13. Registering datasets into Dask-SQL

```
import dask.dataframe as dd
import dask.datasets
from dask_sql import Context

# read dataset
taxi_df = dd.read_csv('./data/taxi_train_subset.csv')
taxi_test = dd.read_csv('./data/taxi_test.csv')

# create a context to register tables
c = Context()
c.create_table("taxi_test", taxi_test)
c.create_table("taxicab", taxi_df)
```

Dask-SQL implements similar ML SQL language to BigQuery ML, allowing you to simply define models, define the training data as a SQL select statement, and then run inference on a different select statement as well.

You can define the model with most of the ML models we discussed, and this will run the scikit-learn ML models in the background. In Example 11-14, we train the LinearRegression model we trained earlier, using Dask-SQL. We first define the

---

model, telling it to use scikit-learn's LinearRegression, and the target column. Then we feed the training data with requisite columns. You can inspect the model trained using the DESCRIBE statement; then you can see in the FROM PREDICT statement how the model is used to run inference on another SQL-defined dataset.

Example 11-14. Defining, training, and predicting a linear regression on Dask-SQL

```
import dask.dataframe as dd
import dask.datasets
from dask_sql import Context

c = Context()
# define model
c.sql(
    """
CREATE MODEL fare_linreg_model WITH (
    model_class = 'LinearRegression',
    wrap_predict = True,
    target_column = 'fare_amount'
) AS (
    SELECT passenger_count, fare_amount
    FROM taxicab
    LIMIT 1000
)
    """
)

# describe model
c.sql(
    """
DESCRIBE MODEL fare_linreg_model
    """
).compute()

# run inference
c.sql(
    """
SELECT
    *
FROM PREDICT(MODEL fare_linreg_model,
    SELECT * FROM taxi_test
)
    """
).compute()
```

Similarly, as shown in Example 11-15, you can run classification models, similar to the XGBoost model we have discussed earlier using the Dask-ML library.

Example 11-15. Defining, training, and predicting a classifier built using XGBoost with Dask-SQL

```
import dask.dataframe as dd
import dask.datasets
from dask_sql import Context

c = Context()
# define model
c.sql(
    """
CREATE MODEL classify_faretype WITH (
    model_class = 'XGBClassifier',
    target_column = 'fare_type'
) AS (
    SELECT airport_surcharge, passenger_count, fare_type
    FROM taxicab
    LIMIT 1000
)
    """
)

# describe model
c.sql(
    """
DESCRIBE MODEL classify_faretype
    """
).compute()

# run inference
c.sql(
    """
SELECT
    *
FROM PREDICT(MODEL classify_faretype,
    SELECT airport_surcharge, passenger_count, FROM taxi_test
)
    """
).compute()
```

Inference and Deployment

Regardless of the libraries chosen to train and validate your model (which could be using some of the Dask-ML libraries, or trained without using Dask at all), here are some of the considerations to keep in mind when using Dask for model inference deployment.

Distributing Data and Models Manually

When loading data and pre-trained models to Dask workers, dask.delayed is the main tool (see Example 11-16). When distributing data, you should choose to use Dask's collections: array and DataFrame. As you recall from Chapter 4, each Dask DataFrame is made up of a pandas DataFrame. This is useful since you can write a method that takes each smaller DataFrame and returns a computed output. Custom functions and tasks can also be given per partition using Dask DataFrame's map _partitions function.

Remember to use delayed notation if you are reading in a large dataset, to delay materialization and avoid reading in unnecessarily early.

 map_partitions passes in a row-wise operation that is meant to be fit into a serializable code that is marshaled to workers. You can define a custom class that handles inference to be called, but a static method needs to be called, not an instance-dependent method. We covered this further in Chapter 4.

Example 11-16. Loading large files on Dask workers

```
from skimage.io import imread
from skimage.io.collection import alphanumeric_key
from dask import delayed
import dask.array as da
import os

root, dirs, filenames = os.walk(dataset_dir)
# sample first file
imread(filenames[0])


@dask.delayed
def lazy_reader(file):
    return imread(file)


# we have a bunch of delayed readers attached to the files
lazy_arrays = [lazy_reader(file) for file in filenames]

# read individual files from reader into a dask array
# particularly useful if each image is a large file like DICOM radiographs
# mammography dicom tends to be extremely large
dask_arrays = [
    da.from_delayed(delayed_reader, shape=(4608, 5200,), dtype=np.float32)
    for delayed_reader in lazy_arrays
]
```

Large-Scale Inferences with Dask

When using Dask for inference on scale, you would distribute trained models to each worker, and then distribute Dask collections (DataFrame or array) over these partitions to work on a portion of the collection at a time, parallelizing the workflow. This strategy would work well in a straightforward inference deployment. We will cover one of the ways to achieve this: defining the workflow manually using `map_partitions`, and then wrapping existing functions with PyTorch or Keras/TensorFlow models. For PyTorch-based models, you can wrap Skorch with the model, which allows it to be used with the Dask-ML API. For TensorFlow models, you would use SciKeras to create a scikit-learn-compatible model, which would allow it to be used for Dask-ML. For PyTorch, the dask-pytorch-ddp library from SaturnCloud is currently the most widely used. As for Keras and TensorFlow, be aware that while it's doable, there are some issues with TensorFlow not liking some of its threads being moved to other workers.

The most generic way to deploy inference is using Dask DataFrame's `map_partitions` (see Example 11-17). You can take your custom inference function that will be run on each row, with the data mapped over each worker by partition.

Example 11-17. Distributed inference using Dask DataFrame

```
import dask.dataframe as dd
import dask.bag as db

def rowwise_operation(row, arg *):
    # row-wise compute
    return result


def partition_operation(df):
    # partition wise logic
    result = df[col1].apply(rowwise_operation)
    return result


ddf = dd.read_csv("metadata_of_files")
results = ddf.map_partitions(partition_operation)
results.compute()

# An alternate way, but note the .apply() here becomes a pandas apply, not
# Dask .apply(), and you must define axis = 1
ddf.map_partitions(
    lambda partition: partition.apply(
        lambda row: rowwise_operation(row), axis=1), meta=(
            'ddf', object))
```

One of the interesting ways that Dask offers more than other scalable libraries is flexibility in parallel behavior. In the preceding example, we define a function that works row-wise and then give that function to a partition-wise logic that will be run by each partition over the entire DataFrame. We can use this as a boilerplate to define more fine-grained batched functions (see Example 11-18). Keep in mind that behaviors you define within the row-wise function should be free of side effects, as in, you should avoid mutating the inputs to the function, as is the general best practice in Dask distributed delayed computations. Also, as the comments in the preceding example say, if you do .apply within a partition-wise lambda, this calls .apply() from pandas. Within Pandas, .apply() defaults to axis = 0, so if you want otherwise, you should remember to specify axis = 1.

Example 11-18. Distributed inference using Dask DataFrame

```
def handle_batch(batch, conn, nlp_model):
    # run_inference_here.
    conn.commit()


def handle_partition(df):
    worker = get_worker()
    conn = connect_to_db()
    try:
        nlp_model = worker.roberta_model
    except BaseException:
        nlp_model = load_model()
        worker.nlp_model = nlp_model
    result, batch = [], []
    for _, row in part.iterrows():
        if len(batch) % batch_size == 0 and len(batch) > 0:
            batch_results = handle_batch(batch, conn, nlp_model)
            result.append(batch_results)
            batch = []
        batch.append((row.doc_id, row.sent_id, row.utterance))
    if len(batch) > 0:
        batch_results = handle_batch(batch, conn, nlp_model)
        result.append(batch_results)
    conn.close()
    return result


ddf = dd.read_csv("metadata.csv")
results = ddf.map_partitions(handle_partition)
results.compute()
```

Conclusion

In this chapter, you have learned how to use the building blocks of Dask to write data science and ML workflows, combining core Dask libraries with other ML libraries you might be familiar with to achieve your desired task. You have also learned how you can use Dask to scale both compute- and memory-bound ML workloads.

Dask-ML provides an almost functionally equivalent library to scikit-learn, often-times calling scikit-learn with the additional awareness of task and data parallelism that Dask brings. Dask-ML is actively being developed by the community and will evolve to add more use cases and examples. Check the Dask documentation for the latest updates.

In addition, you have learned methods of parallelizing ML training with models from scikit-learn libraries by using joblib for compute-intensive workloads, and batched operations for data-intensive workloads, so that you can write any custom implementations yourself.

Finally, you have learned the use cases for Dask-SQL and its SQL ML statements in providing high-level abstraction for model creation, hyperparameter tuning, and inference.

Since ML can be very computation- and memory-heavy, it's important to deploy your ML work on a correctly configured cluster and monitor the progress and output closely. We will cover deployment, profiling, and troubleshooting in the next chapter.

## CHAPTER 12

Productionizing Dask: Notebooks, Deployment, Tuning, and Monitoring

We have bundled most of the things we believe are going to be critical for you to move from your laptop into production in this chapter. Notebooks and deployments go together, as Dask's notebook interface greatly simplifies many aspects of using its distributed deployments. While you don't need to use notebooks to access Dask, and in many cases notebooks have serious drawbacks (*https://oreil.ly/oi09S*), for interactive use cases it's often hard to beat the trade-offs. Interactive/exploratory work has a way of becoming permanent mission-critical workflows, and we cover the steps necessary to turn exploratory work into production deployments.

You can deploy Dask in many fashions, from running it on top of other distributed compute engines like Ray to deploying it on YARN or a raw collection of machines. Once you've got your Dask job deployed, you'll likely need to tune it so you don't use your company's entire AWS budget on one job. And then, finally, before you can walk away from a job, you'll need to set up monitoring—so you know when it's broken.

 If you're just here to learn how to use Dask with notebooks, feel free to skip ahead to that section. If you want to learn more about deploying Dask, congratulations and condolences on exceeding the scale you can handle on a single computer.

In this chapter, we will cover some (but not all) of the deployment options for Dask and their trade-offs. You will learn how to integrate notebooks into the most common deployment environments. You'll see how to use these notebooks to track the progress of your Dask tasks and access the Dask UI when running remotely. We will finish by covering some options for deploying your scheduled tasks, so you can take a vacation without lining up someone to press run on your notebook every day.

This chapter covers Dask's distributed deployments, but if your Dask program is happy in local mode, don't feel the need to deploy a cluster just for the sake of it.[1]

Factors to Consider in a Deployment Option

When you are choosing how to deploy Dask, there are many different factors to consider, but often the biggest one is what tools your organization is already using. Most of the deployment options map to different types of cluster managers (CMs). CMs manage sets of computers and provide some isolation between users and jobs. Isolation can be incredibly important—for example, if one user eats all of the candy (or CPU), then another user won't have any candy. Most cluster managers provide CPU and memory isolation, and some also isolate other resources (like disks and GPUs). Most clouds (AWS, GCP, etc.) offer both Kubernetes and YARN cluster managers, which can dynamically scale the number of nodes up and down. Dask does not need a CM to run, but without one, auto-scaling and other important features are not available.

When choosing a deployment mechanism, with or without a CM, some important factors to consider are the ability to scale up and down, multi-tenancy, dependency management, and whether the deployment method supports heterogeneous workers.

The ability to scale up and down (or *dynamic scale*) is important in many situations, as computers cost money. Heterogeneous or mixed worker types are important for workloads that take advantage of accelerators (like GPUs), so that non-accelerated work can be scheduled on less-expensive nodes. Support for heterogeneous workers goes well with dynamic scaling, as the workers can be replaced.

Multi-tenancy can reduce wasted compute resources for systems that cannot scale up and down.

Dependency management allows you to control, at runtime or in advance, what software is on the workers. This is critical in Dask; if the workers and the client do not have the same libraries, your code may not function. Additionally, some libraries can be slow to install at runtime, so the ability to pre-install or share an environment can be beneficial for some use cases, especially those in deep learning.

Table 12-1 compares some of the deployment options in Dask.

---

[1] We don't (currently) work for cloud providers, so if your workload fits on your laptop, more power to you. Just remember to use source control. If possible, though, putting it on a server can be a useful exercise for capturing the dependencies and ensuring your production environment can survive the loss of a laptop.

Table 12-1. Deployment option comparisons

Deployment method	Dynamic scale	Recommended use case[a]	Dependency management	Notebook deployed inside[b]	Mixed worker types
localhost	No	Testing, solo dev, GPU-only acceleration	Yes (runtime or pre-install)	Yes	No
ssh	No	Solo lab, testing, but generally not recommended (k8s instead)	Runtime only	Yes	Yes (manual)
Slurm + GW	Yes	Existing high-performance computing/Slurm environments	Yes (runtime or pre-install)	Separate project	Varies
Dask "Cloud"	Yes	Not recommended; use Dask + K8s or YARN on cloud provider	Runtime only	Medium effort[c]	No
Dask + K8s	Yes	Cloud environments, existing K8s deployments	Runtime or pre-install (but more effort)	Separate project, medium effort	Yes
Dask + YARN	Yes	Existing big data deployments	Runtime or pre-install (but more effort)	Separate project that has not been updated since 2019	Yes
Dask + Ray + [CM]	Depends on CM	Existing Ray deployments, multi-tool (TF, etc.), or actor systems	Depends on CM (always at least runtime)	Depends on CM	Yes
Coiled	yes	New cloud deployments	Yes, including magic "auto-sync"	No	Yes

[a] This is largely based on our experiences and may be biased toward large companies and academic environments. Please feel free to make your own call.

[b] There are some workarounds (*https://oreil.ly/TqhBb*).

[c] Some large commodity cloud providers were easier than others. Mika's own experience ranks Google Cloud as easiest, Amazon as moderate, and Azure as hardest to work with. Google Cloud has a good working guide on using Dask with RAPIDS NVIDIA architecture and a well-documented workflow. Amazon Web Services similarly has good documentation on running Dask workers on multiple Amazon Elastic Compute Cloud (EC2) instances and a guide on attaching S3 buckets. Azure needed some work to make worker provisioning work well, mostly due to its environment and user provisioning workflow being a bit different from that of AWS or GCP.

Building Dask on a Kubernetes Deployment

There are two main ways to deploy Dask on Kubernetes:[2] KubeCluster and HelmCluster. Helm is a popular tool for managing deployments on Kubernetes, with the deployments being specified in Helm charts. Since Helm is the newer recommended way of managing deployments on Kubernetes, we will cover that one here.

The Helm documentation (*https://oreil.ly/EBzBm*) offers an excellent starting point on the different ways to install Helm, but for those in a hurry, `curl https://raw.githubusercontent.com/helm/helm/main/scripts/get-helm-3 | bash` will do it for you.[3]

 The Dask on Kubernetes Helm chart deploys what is called an *operator*. Currently, installing operators requires the ability to install Custom Resource Definitions (CRDs) and may require administrator privileges. If you can't get the permissions (or someone with the permissions), you can still use the "vanilla" or "classic" deployment mode (*https://oreil.ly/-MLRk*).

Since GPU resources are costly, it is typical to want to allocate only as many of them as needed. Some cluster manager interfaces, including Dask's Kubernetes plug-in, allow you to configure multiple types of workers so that Dask will allocate GPU workers only when needed. On our Kubernetes cluster, we deploy the Dask operator as shown in Example 12-1.

Example 12-1. Deploying the Dask operator with Helm

```
# Add the repo
helm repo add dask https://helm.dask.org
helm repo update
# Install the operator; you will use this to create clusters
helm install --create-namespace -n \
     dask-operator --generate-name dask/dask-kubernetes-operator
```

---

2 PEP20's view on the obvious way to do things remains a suggestion more observed in the breach.

3 Note this installs Helm 3.X. As with Python 3, Helm 3 has a large number of breaking changes over Helm 2 (*https://oreil.ly/vR5BM*), so when you're reading documentation (or installing packages), make sure it's referencing the current major versions.

Now you can use the Dask operator either by creating YAML files (likely not your favorite) or with the KubeCluster API, as shown in Example 12-2, where we create a cluster and then add additional worker types, allowing Dask to create two different kinds of workers.[4]

Example 12-2. Using the Dask operator

```
from dask_kubernetes.operator import KubeCluster

cluster = KubeCluster(name='simple',
                      n_workers=1,
                      resources={
                          "requests": {"memory": "16Gi"},
                          "limits": {"memory": "16Gi"}
                      })

cluster.add_worker_group(name="highmem",
                         n_workers=0,
                         resources={
                             "requests": {"memory": "64Gi"},
                             "limits": {"memory": "64Gi"}
                         })

cluster.add_worker_group(name="gpu",
                         n_workers=0,
                         resources={
                             "requests": {"nvidia.com/gpu": "1"},
                             "limits": {"nvidia.com/gpu": "1"}
                         })
# Now you can scale these worker groups up and down as needed
cluster.scale("gpu", 5, worker_group="gpu")
# Fancy machine learning logic
cluster.scale("gpu", , worker_group="gpu")
# Or just auto-scale
cluster.adapt(minimum=1, maximum=10)
```

In 2020 Dask added a DaskHub Helm chart (*https://oreil.ly/otOQX*), which combines the deployment of JupyterHub with the Dask Gateway.

---

4 Mixed worker types; see "Worker Resources" (*https://oreil.ly/O52ib*) in the Dask documentation and the blog article "How to Run Different Worker Types with the Dask Helm Chart" (*https://oreil.ly/mJR6b*).

Dask on Ray

Deploying Dask on Ray is a little bit different than all of the other options, in that it changes not only how Dask workers and tasks are scheduled but also how Dask objects are stored (*https://oreil.ly/PIwuX*). This can reduce the number of copies of the same object that need to be stored, allowing you to use your cluster memory more efficiently.

If you have a Ray deployment available to you, enabling Dask can be incredibly straightforward, as shown in Example 12-3.

Example 12-3. Running Dask on Ray

```
import dask

enable_dask_on_ray()
ddf_students = ray.data.dataset.Dataset.to_dask(ray_dataset)
ddf_students.head()

disable_dask_on_ray()
```

However, if you don't have an existing Ray cluster, you will still need to deploy Ray somewhere with the same considerations as Dask. Deploying Ray is beyond the scope of this book. Ray's production guide (*https://oreil.ly/PNb0_*) has details for deploying on Ray, as does *Scaling Python with Ray*.

Dask on YARN

YARN is a popular cluster manager from the big data world that is available in open source as well as commercial on-premises (e.g., Cloudera) and cloud (e.g., Elastic Map Reduce). There are two ways to run Dask on a YARN cluster: one is with Dask-Yarn, and the other is with Dask-Gateway. While the two methods are similar, Dask-Gateway is potentially a bit more involved, as it adds a centrally managed server that runs to manage Dask clusters, but it has more fine-grained security and administrative controls.

Depending on the cluster, your workers might be more transient than other types, and their IP address might not be static when they get spun up again. You should ensure worker/scheduler service discovery methods are put in place for your own cluster setup. It could be as simple as a shared file that they read from, or a more resilient broker. If no additional arguments are given, Dask workers would use the `DASK_SCHEDULER_ADDRESS` environment variable to connect.

Example 12-4 expands on Example 9-1 with a custom conda environment and logging framework.

Example 12-4. Deploying Dask on YARN with a custom conda environment

```python
from dask_yarn import YarnCluster
from dask.distributed import Client
import logging
import os
import sys
import time

logger = logging.getLogger(__name__)

WORKER_ENV = {
    "HADOOP_CONF_DIR": "/data/app/spark-yarn/hadoop-conf",
    "JAVA_HOME": "/usr/lib/jvm/java"}

logging.basicConfig(
    level=logging.DEBUG,
    format="%(asctime)s %(levelname)s %(name)s: %(message)s")

logger.info("Initializing YarnCluster")
cluster_start_time = time.time()

# say your desired conda environment for workers is located at
# /home/mkimmins/anaconda/bin/python
# similar syntax for venv and python executable
cluster = YarnCluster(
    environment='conda:///home/mkimmins/anaconda/bin/python',
    worker_vcores=2,
    worker_memory="4GiB")

logger.info(
    "Initializing YarnCluster: done in %.4f",
    time.time() -
    cluster_start_time)

logger.info("Initializing Client")
client = Client(cluster)
logger.info(
    "Initializing Client: done in %.4f",
    time.time() -
    client_start_time)

# Important and common misconfig is mismatched versions on nodes
versions = dask_client.get_versions(check=True)
```

Alternatively, you can run the cluster with the CLI interface that Dask-Yarn exposes. You would first deploy YARN in the shell script of your choosing; the shell script then invokes the Python file you want to run. Within the Python file, you reference the deployed YARN cluster, as shown in Example 12-5. This can be an easier way to chain your jobs and inspect and pull logs. Note that the CLI is supported only in Python versions above 2.7.6.

Example 12-5. Deploying Dask on YARN with CLI interface

```
get_ipython().system('dask-yarn submit')

'''
--environment home/username/anaconda/bin/python --worker-count 20 \
--worker-vcores 2 --worker-memory 4GiB your_python_script.py
'''

# Since we already deployed and ran YARN cluster,
# we replace YarnCluster(...) with from_current() to reference it
cluster = YarnCluster.from_current()

# This would give you YARN application ID
# application_1516806604516_0019
# status check, kill, view log of application
get_ipython().system('dask-yarn status application_1516806604516_0019')
get_ipython().system('dask-yarn kill application_1516806604516_0019')
get_ipython().system('yarn logs -applicationId application_1516806604516_0019')
```

Dask on High-Performance Computing

Dask has gained a big academic and scientific user base. This comes in part from how you can use existing high-performance computing (HPC) clusters with Dask to make readily available scalable scientific computing without rewriting all of your code.[5]

You can turn your HPC account into a high-performance Dask environment that you can connect to from Jupyter on your local machine. Dask uses its Dask-jobqueue library to support many HPC cluster types, including HTCondor, LSF, Moab, OAR, PBS, SGE, TORQUE, DRMAA, and Slurm. A separate library, Dask-MPI, supports MPI clusters. In Example 9-2, we showed a sample of how to use Dask on Slurm, and in the following section, we'll build on that example.

Setting Up Dask in a Remote Cluster

The first step for using Dask on your cluster is to set up your own Python and iPython environments in the cluster. The exact way to do that will vary by your cluster's admin's preferences. Generally, users often use virtualenv (*https://oreil.ly/mLAOj*) or miniconda (*https://oreil.ly/zXsTP*) to install related libraries on a user level. Miniconda makes it easier to use not just your own libraries but your own version of Python. Once that is done, ensure your Python command points to

---

5 In some ways, HPC and cluster managers are different names for the same thing, with cluster managers coming out of industry and HPC out of research. HPC clusters tend to have and use a shared network storage that is not as common in industry.

the Python binary in your user space by running which python or installing and importing a library not available in system Python.

The Dask-jobqueue library converts your Dask settings and configurations into a job script that is submitted to the HPC cluster. The following example starts a cluster with Slurm workers, and the semantics are similar for other HPC API. Dask-MPI uses a slightly different pattern, so be sure to refer to its documentation for details. job_directives_skip is an optional parameter, used to ignore errors in cases where auto-generated job script inserts some commands that your particular cluster does not recognize. job_script_prologue is also an optional parameter that specifies shell commands to be run at each worker spawn. This is a good place to ensure proper Python environments are set up, or a cluster-specific setup script.

Make sure HPC cluster specs for worker memory and cores are correctly matched in resource_spec arguments, which are given to your HPC system itself to request the workers. The former is used for the Dask scheduler to set its internals; the latter is for you to request the resource within the HPC.

HPC systems often leverage high-performance network interface on top of a standard Ethernet network, and this has become a crucial way to speed up data movement. You can pass an optional interface parameter, as shown in Example 12-6, to instruct Dask to use the higher-bandwidth network. If you are not sure which interfaces are available, type in ifconfig on your terminal, and it will show infiniband, often ib0, as one of the available network interfaces.

Finally, the cores and memory description are per-worker resources, and n_workers specifies how many jobs you want to queue initially. You can scale and add more workers after the fact, as we do in Example 12-6, with the cluster.scale() command.

Some HPC systems use GB when they mean 1,024-based units. Dask-jobqueue sticks with the proper notation of GiB. 1 GB is $1,000^3$ bytes, and 1 GiB is $1,024^3$ bytes. Academic settings often use binary measurements, while commercial settings usually opt for SI units, hence the discrepancy.

Before running Dask in a new environment, you should check the job script that is auto-generated by Dask-jobqueue for unsupported commands. While Dask's job-queue library tries to work with many HPC systems, it may not have all of the quirks of your institution's setup. If you are familiar with the cluster capabilities, you may find unsupported commands by calling print(cluster.job_script()). You can also try to run a small version of your job first with a limited number of workers and see where they fail. If you find any issues with the script, you should use the job_directives_skip parameter to skip the unsupported components, as outlined in Example 12-6.

Example 12-6. Deploying Dask on an HPC cluster by hand

```
from dask_jobqueue import SLURMCluster
from dask.distributed import Client


def create_slurm_clusters(cores, processes, workers, memory="16GB",
                          queue='regular', account="account", username="user"):
    cluster = SLURMCluster(
        #ensure walltime request is reasonable within your specific cluster
        walltime="04:00:00",
        queue=queue,
        account=account,
        cores=cores,
        processes=processes,
        memory=memory,
        worker_extra_args=["--resources GPU=1"],
        job_extra=['--gres=gpu:1'],
        job_directives_skip=['--mem', 'another-string'],
        job_script_prologue=[
            '/your_path/pre_run_script.sh',
            'source venv/bin/activate'],
        interface='ib0',
        log_directory='dask_slurm_logs',
        python=f'srun -n 1 -c {processes} python',
        local_directory=f'/dev/{username}',
        death_timeout=300
    )
    cluster.start_workers(workers)
    return cluster


cluster = create_slurm_clusters(cores=4, processes=1, workers=4)
cluster.scale(10)
client = Client(cluster)
```

In Example 12-7 we tie together many of the concepts we've introduced. Here we run a delayed execution over some asynchronous task using Dask delayed, which is deployed on a Slurm cluster. The example also combines several logging strategies we've mentioned, such as revealing the underlying deployment HPC job script, as well as providing a progress bar for users to track in a notebook or in their CLI of choice.

Example 12-7. Deploying Dask using jobqueue over Slurm with Dask futures

```
import time
from dask import delayed
from dask.distributed import Client, LocalCluster
# Note we introduce progress bar for future execution in a distributed
# context here
from dask.distributed import progress
from dask_jobqueue import SLURMCluster
import numpy as np
import logging

logger = logging.getLogger(__name__)
logging.basicConfig(
    level=logging.DEBUG,
    format="%(asctime)s %(levelname)s %(name)s: %(message)s")


def visit_url(i):
    return "Some fancy operation happened. Trust me."


@delayed
def crawl(url, depth=0, maxdepth=1, maxlinks=4):
    # some complicated and async job
    # refer to Chapter 2 for full implementation of crawl
    time.sleep(1)
    some_output = visit_url(url)
    return some_output


def main_event(client):
    njobs = 100
    outputs = []
    for i in range(njobs):
        # assume we have a queue of work to do
        url = work_queue.deque()
        output = crawl(url)
        outputs.append(output)

    results = client.persist(outputs)
    logger.info(f"Running main loop...")
    progress(results)


def cli():
    cluster = create_slurm_clusters(cores=10, processes=10, workers=2)
    logger.info(f"Submitting SLURM job with jobscript: {cluster.job_script()}")
    client = Client(cluster)
    main_event(client)
```

```
if __name__ == "__main__":
    logger.info("Initializing SLURM Cluster")
    cli()
```

 Always ensure your walltime requests don't run afoul of HPC resource managers. For example, Slurm has a backfill scheduler that applies its own logic, and if you request too long a walltime, your request for compute resources can get stuck in the queue, unable to spin up on time. In such a case, the Dask client may error out with a non-descriptive message, such as "Failed to start worker process. Restarting." At the time of writing, there aren't many ways to surface specific deployment issues without some logging code from the user end.

On the more advanced end, you can control your cluster configuration by updating the Dask-jobqueue YAML file, which is generated on first run and stored at /.config/dask/jobqueue.yaml. The jobqueue configuration file contains, commented out, default configurations for many different types of clusters. To get started editing the file, uncomment the cluster type you are using (e.g., Slurm), and then you can change the values to meet your specific needs. The jobqueue configuration file allows you to configure additional parameters not available through the Python constructor.

If Dask starts to run out of memory, it will by default start to write data out to disk (called spill-to-disk). This is normally great, since we tend to have more disk than memory, and while it is slower, it's not that much slower. However, on HPC environments, the default location that Dask may write to could be a network storage drive, which will be as slow as transferring the data on the network. You should make sure Dask writes to local storage. You can ask your cluster administrator for the local scratch directory or use df -h to see where different storage devices are mapped. If you don't have local storage available, or if it's too small, you can also turn off spill-to-disk. Both disabling and changing the location of spill-to-disk on clusters can be configured in the ~/.config/dask/distributed.yaml file (also created on first run).

 Adaptive scaling is a great way to scale your job up and down while your application is running, especially on busy shared machines like HPC systems. However, each HPC system is unique, and sometimes the way Dask-jobqueue handles adaptive scaling creates issues. We have encountered such a problem when running Dask adaptive scaling on Slurm using jobqueue but with some effort were able to configure it properly.

Dask also uses files for locking, which can cause issues when using a shared network drive, as is common in HPC clusters. If there are multiple workers working simultaneously, it uses a locking mechanism, which excludes another process from accessing this file, to orchestrate itself. Some issues on HPC can come down to an incomplete locking transaction, or an inability to write a file on disk due to administrative restrictions. Worker configs can be toggled to disable this behavior.

Cluster parameters, such as memory allocation and number of jobs, workers, processes, and CPUs per task, are quite sensitive to user input and can be difficult to grasp at the beginning. For example, if you launch an HPC cluster with multiple processes, each process will take a fraction of total allocated memory. Ten processes with 30 GB of memory would mean each process gets 3 GB of memory. If your workflow at peak has more than 95% of the process memory (2.85 GB in our example), your process will be paused and even terminated early due to memory overflow risks, potentially resulting in a failed task. For more on memory management, refer to "Worker Memory Management" on page 167.

For HPC users, most processes you launch will have a limited amount of walltime that the job is allowed to stay on. You can stagger the creation of workers in such a way that you will have at least one worker running at all times, creating an infinite worker loop. Alternatively, you can also stagger the creation and end of the workers, so that you avoid all of the workers ending simultaneously. Example 12-8 shows you how.

Example 12-8. Dask worker management through adaptive scaling

```
from dask_jobqueue import SLURMCluster
from dask import delayed
from dask.distributed import Client

#we give walltime of 4 hours to the cluster spawn
#each Dask worker is told they have 5 min less than that for Dask to manage
#we tell workers to stagger their start and close in a random interval of 5 min
# some workers will die, but others will be staggered alive, avoiding loss
# of job

cluster = SLURMCluster(
    walltime="04:00:00",
    cores=24,
    processes=6,
    memory="8gb",
    #args passed directly to worker
    worker_extra_args=["--lifetime", "235m", "--lifetime-stagger", "5m"],
    #path to the interpreter that you want to run the batch submission script
    shebang='#!/usr/bin/env zsh',
```

```
    #path to desired python runtime if you have a separate one
    python='~/miniconda/bin/python'
)

client = Client(cluster)
```

> Different workers can have different startup times, as well as con-
> tain different amounts of data, which impacts the cost of fault
> recovery.

While Dask has good tools to monitor its own behavior, sometimes the integration
between Dask and your HPC cluster (or other cluster) can break. If you suspect
jobqueue isn't sending the right worker commands for your particular cluster, you
can inspect the *./config/dask/jobqueue.yaml* file directly or dynamically at runtime or
in your Jupyter notebook by running `config.get('jobqueue.yaml')`.

Connecting a Local Machine to an HPC Cluster

Part of running Dask remotely is being able to connect to the server to run your
tasks. If you want to connect your client to a remote cluster, run Jupyter remotely, or
just access the UI on a cluster, you'll need to be able to connect to some ports on the
remote machine.

> Another option is to have Dask bind to a public IP address, but
> without careful firewall rules, this means that anyone can access
> your Dask cluster, which is likely not your intention.

In HPC environments you often already connect using SSH, so using SSH port
forwarding is often the easiest way to connect. SSH port forwarding allows you to
map a port on another computer to one on your local computer.[6] The default Dask
monitoring port is 8787, but if that port is busy (or you configure a different one),
Dask may bind to a different port. The Dask server prints out which ports it is bound
to at start time. To forward port 8787 on a remote machine to the same local port,
you could run `ssh -L localhost:8787:my-awesome-hpc-node.hpc.fake:8787`. You
can use the same techniques (but with different port numbers) for a remote Jupyter-
Lab, or to connect a Dask client to a remote scheduler.

---

6 You can also run an SSH socks proxy, which makes it easy to access other servers inside the HPC cluster, but
  which also requires changing your browser configuration (and does not work for the Dask client).

If you want to leave a process running remotely (like JupyterLab), the screen command can be a great way of having a process last beyond a single session.

With the immense popularity of notebooks, some HPC clusters have special tools to make it even easier to launch Jupyter notebooks. We recommend looking for your cluster administrator's documentation on how to launch Jupyter notebooks, as you may accidentally create security issues if you don't do it correctly.

Dask JupyterLab Extension and Magics

You can run Dask in Jupyter like any other library, but Dask's JupyterLab extensions make it easier to understand the status of your Dask job while it's running.

Installing JupyterLab Extensions

Dask's lab extensions require `nodejs`, which can be installed with `conda install -c conda-forge nodejs`. If you are not using conda, it can also be installed with `brew install node` on Apple or `sudo apt install nodejs` on Ubuntu.

Dask's lab extensions package is available as `dask-labextension`.

Once you've installed the lab extension, it will show up with the Dask logo on the left side, as shown in Figure 12-1.

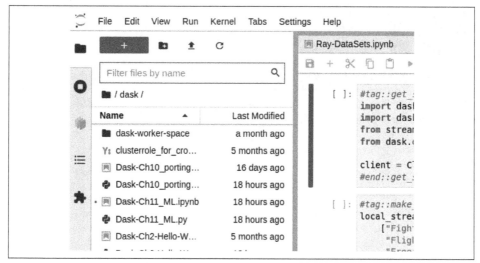

Figure 12-1. A successfully deployed Dask instance on JupyterLab (digital, color version: https://oreil.ly/TlOSc)

Launching Clusters

From there you can launch your cluster. By default, the extension launches a local cluster, but you can configure it to use different deployment options, including Kubernetes, by editing *~/.config/dask*.

UI

If you are using Dask's JupyterLab extension (see Figure 12-2), it provides a link to the cluster UI as well as the ability to drag individual components into the Jupyter interface.

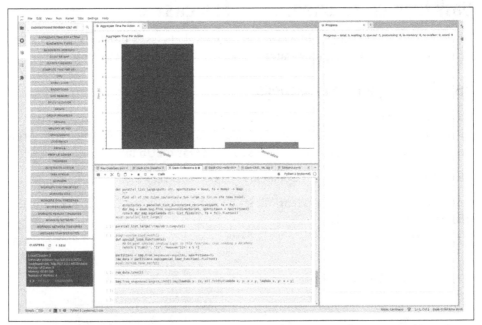

Figure 12-2. Dask web UI inside JupyterHub using the JupyterLab extension (digital, color version: https://oreil.ly/5UOHI)

The JupyterLab extension links to the Dask web UI, and you can also get a link through the cluster's repr. If the cluster link does not work/is not accessible, you can try installing the jupyter-server-proxy extension so you can use the notebook host as a jump host (*https://oreil.ly/0eIhP*).

Watching Progress

Dask jobs tend to take a long time to run; otherwise we would not be putting in the effort to parallelize them. You can use Dask's progress function from dask.distrib uted to track your futures' progress inside your notebook itself (see Figure 12-3).

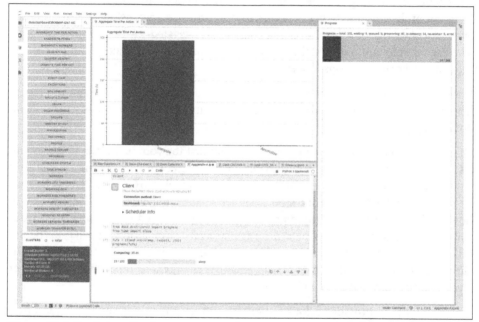

Figure 12-3. Real-time Dask progress monitoring in JupyterHub (digital, color version: https://oreil.ly/amaBq)

Understanding Dask Performance

Tuning your Dask program involves understanding the intersection of many components. You will need to understand your code's behavior and how it interacts with the data given and the machines. You can use Dask metrics to gain insight on much of this, but, especially if you did not create it, it's important to look at the program as well.

Metrics in Distributed Computing

Distributed computing requires constantly making decisions and weighing the optimization of the cost and benefits of distributing workload against locally running the work. Most of that low-level decision making is delegated to the internals of Dask. The user should still monitor the runtime characteristics and make modifications to the code and configurations if needed.

Dask automatically tracks relevant compute and runtime metrics. You can use this to help you decide how to store your data, as well as inform where to focus your time on optimizing your code.

Of course, the cost of computation is more than just the compute time. Users should also consider the time spent transferring data over network, the memory footprint within the workers, GPU/CPU utilization rate, and disk I/O costs. These in turn let you understand the higher-level insights of data movement and computation flow, such as how much of the memory in a worker is used up in storing previous computation that hasn't been passed on to the next computation, or what particular function is taking up the most amount of time. Monitoring these can help tune your cluster and code, but it also can help identify emergent computation patterns or logical bottlenecks that you can change.

Dask's dashboard provides a lot of statistics and graphs to answer these questions. The dashboard is a web page tied to your Dask cluster at runtime. You can access it through your local machine or on the remote machine that it is running in, through methods we discussed earlier in this chapter. Here, we will cover a few of the ways you can get insights from the performance metrics and tune Dask accordingly to achieve better results.

The Dask Dashboard

Dask's dashboard contains many different pages, each of which can help with understanding different parts of your program.

Task stream

The Task Stream dashboard gives a high-level view of each worker and its behavior. Exact methods invoked are color-coded, and you can inspect them by zooming in and out. Each row represents one worker. The custom-colored bars are user-induced tasks, and there are four preset colors to indicate common worker tasks: data transfer between workers, disk read and writes, serialization and deserialization times, and failed tasks. Figure 12-4 shows a compute workload that is distributed over 10 workers and is well balanced, with no one worker finishing late, evenly distributed compute time, and minimal network IO overhead.

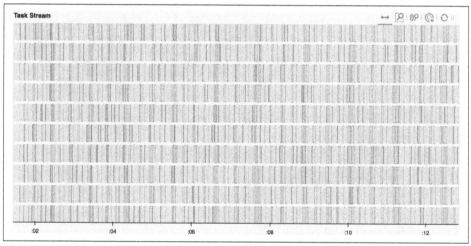

Figure 12-4. A task stream with well-balanced workers (digital, color version: https://oreil.ly/VbpGF)

On the other hand, Figure 12-5 shows a situation in which compute is uneven. You can see that there is a lot of whitespace between computation, meaning the workers are blocked and are not actually computing during that time. Additionally, you see some workers start earlier and others finish later, hinting that there are some issues with distributing the job. This could be due to the inherent dependency of your code or suboptimal tuning. Changing the DataFrame or array chunk sizes might make these less fragmented. You do see that when the job starts on each worker, they take roughly the same amount of work, meaning the work itself is still balanced fairly well and distributing the workload is giving you good returns. This is a fairly contrived illustrative example, so this task only took a few seconds, but the same idea applies to longer and bulkier workloads as well.

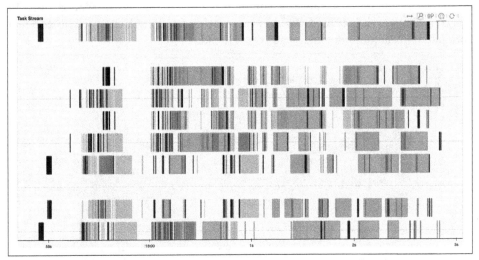

Figure 12-5. A task stream with too many small data chunks (digital, color version: https://oreil.ly/oI2ab)

Memory

You can monitor the memory usage, sometimes referred to as *memory pressure*,[7] of each worker on the Bytes Stored portion (see Figure 12-6). These are by default color-coded to signify memory pressure within limits, approaching limit, and spilled to disk. Even if memory usage is within the limits, as it increases beyond 60% to 70%, you are likely to encounter performance slowdowns. Since memory usage is rising, internals of Python and Dask are going to run costlier garbage collection and memory optimization tasks in the background to keep it from rising.

---

7 You can think of the memory as a balloon that we fill up, and as we get higher pressure it's more likely to have issues. It's a bit of a stretch as a metaphor, we admit.

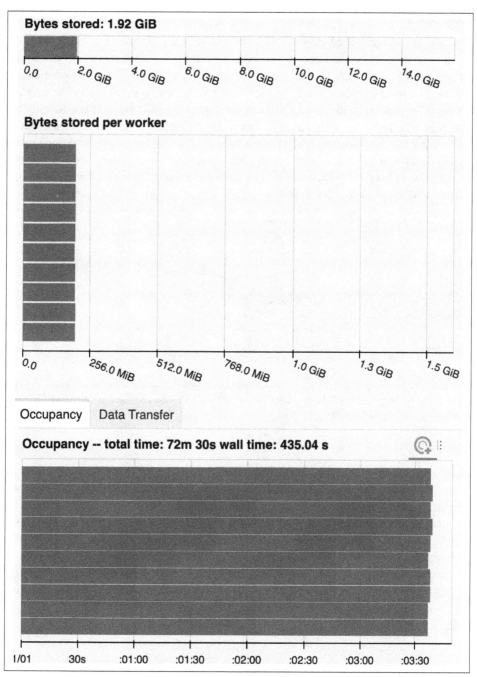

Figure 12-6. Memory usage by worker in the monitoring UI (digital, color version: https://oreil.ly/9GfNp)

Task progress

You can see the aggregated view of task completion in the progress bar in Figure 12-7. The order of execution is from top to bottom, although that does not always mean it's completely sequential. The colors of the bars are particularly information-rich for tuning. The solid gray on the far right for sum() and random_sample() in Figure 12-7 means tasks that are ready to run, with dependent data ready but not yet assigned to a worker. The bold non-gray colors mean tasks are finished, with result data that is waiting for the next sequence of tasks to take it. The fainter non-gray color blocks signify tasks that are done, with result data handed off and purged from memory. Your goal is to keep the solid-color blocks within a manageable size, to make sure you utilize most of your allocated memory.

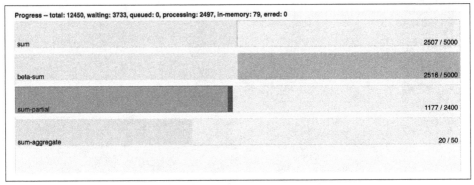

Figure 12-7. Progress monitoring by task, summed over all workers (digital, color version: https://oreil.ly/v8XoP)

Task graph

Similar information is available on Task Graph (see Figure 12-8), from the view of individual tasks. You may be familiar with these types of MapReduce-like directed acyclic graphs. Order of computation is shown from left to right, with your tasks originating from many parallel workloads, distributed among your workers, and ending up with an outcome that is distributed among 10 workers, in this case. This graph is also an accurate low-level depiction of task dependencies. The color coding also highlights where in the computational life cycle each work and data is currently sitting in. By looking at this, you can get a sense of which tasks are bottlenecks and thus are potentially good places to start optimizing your code.

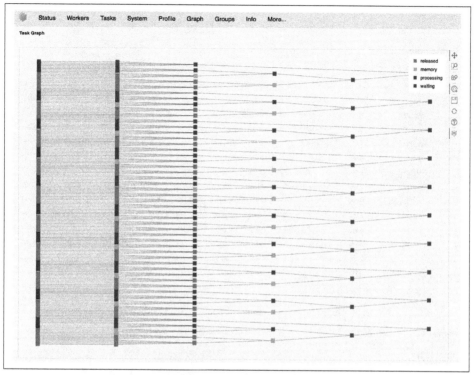

Figure 12-8. A task graph showing the color-coded status of each task and its preceding and succeeding tasks (digital, color version: https://oreil.ly/RSBiv)

The Workers tab allows you to see real-time CPU, memory, and disk IO, among other things (see Figure 12-9). Monitoring this tab can be useful if you suspect that your worker is running out of memory or disk space. Some of the remedies for that can include allocating more memory to the workers or choosing a different chunking size or method for the data.

Figure 12-10 shows worker event monitoring. Dask's distributed scheduler runs on a loop called event loop, which manages all tasks that are to be scheduled and the workers, managing the execution, communication, and status of the computation. The event_loop_interval metric is a measure of average time between the iterations of this loop for each worker. A shorter time means it took less time for the scheduler to do its management tasks for this worker. If this goes higher, this could mean a number of things, including suboptimal network configuration, resource contention, or high communication overhead. If this remains high, you might want to look into whether you have enough resources for the compute, and either allocate larger resources per worker or rechunk the data into smaller portions.

name	address	nthreads	cpu	memory	limit	memory %	managed	unmanage	unmanage	spilled	# fds	net read	net write
Total (10)		10	60 %	1.9 GiB	16.0 GiB	11.8 %	695.3 KiB	1.9 GiB	9.4 MiB	0.0	326	2 MiB	2 MiB
0	tcp://127.0. 1		59 %	193.7 MiB	1.6 GiB	11.8 %	85.9 KiB	192.6 MiB	996.0 KiB	0.0	33	192 KiB	192 KiB
1	tcp://127.0. 1		57 %	190.9 MiB	1.6 GiB	11.7 %	70.3 KiB	190.0 MiB	879.8 KiB	0.0	33	198 KiB	198 KiB
2	tcp://127.0. 1		58 %	193.5 MiB	1.6 GiB	11.8 %	62.5 KiB	192.4 MiB	1.0 MiB	0.0	33	192 KiB	192 KiB
3	tcp://127.0. 1		62 %	194.2 MiB	1.6 GiB	11.9 %	70.3 KiB	193.2 MiB	883.8 KiB	0.0	31	192 KiB	192 KiB
4	tcp://127.0. 1		58 %	192.0 MiB	1.6 GiB	11.7 %	70.3 KiB	191.1 MiB	852.0 KiB	0.0	31	192 KiB	192 KiB
5	tcp://127.0. 1		62 %	192.8 MiB	1.6 GiB	11.8 %	62.5 KiB	191.8 MiB	1011.3 KiB	0.0	39	206 KiB	206 KiB
6	tcp://127.0. 1		66 %	194.9 MiB	1.6 GiB	11.9 %	70.3 KiB	193.9 MiB	867.8 KiB	0.0	31	172 KiB	170 KiB
7	tcp://127.0. 1		57 %	193.5 MiB	1.6 GiB	11.8 %	70.3 KiB	192.5 MiB	951.4 KiB	0.0	31	182 KiB	182 KiB
8	tcp://127.0. 1		64 %	194.5 MiB	1.6 GiB	11.9 %	70.3 KiB	193.4 MiB	1007.8 KiB	0.0	31	174 KiB	172 KiB
9	tcp://127.0. 1		60 %	193.8 MiB	1.6 GiB	11.8 %	62.5 KiB	192.7 MiB	1.1 MiB	0.0	33	204 KiB	204 KiB

Figure 12-9. Worker monitoring for a Dask cluster with 10 workers (digital, color version: https://oreil.ly/QlDQE)

name	address	event_loop_interval	disk read	disk write
Total (10)		0.19999192237854005	14 MiB	14 MiB
0	tcp://127.0.0.1:56040	0.020010418891906738	879 KiB	72 KiB
1	tcp://127.0.0.1:56028	0.01999070167541504	2 MiB	2 MiB
2	tcp://127.0.0.1:56025	0.02000108242034912	2 MiB	2 MiB
3	tcp://127.0.0.1:56043	0.02000393867492676	880 KiB	72 KiB
4	tcp://127.0.0.1:56022	0.019987421035766603	2 MiB	2 MiB
5	tcp://127.0.0.1:56031	0.020019798278808593	2 MiB	232 KiB
6	tcp://127.0.0.1:56019	0.019994702339172363	2 MiB	2 MiB
7	tcp://127.0.0.1:56037	0.020004701614379884	840 KiB	3 MiB
8	tcp://127.0.0.1:56016	0.019980678558349608	8 KiB	663 KiB
9	tcp://127.0.0.1:56034	0.019999847888946533	2 MiB	224 KiB

Figure 12-10. Worker event monitoring for a Dask cluster (digital, color version: https://oreil.ly/vU6lG)

The System tab allows you to track the CPU, memory, network bandwidth, and file descriptors. CPU and memory are easy to understand. An HPC user would be keen to track network bandwidth if their job requires heavy amounts of data to be moved around. File descriptors here track the number of input and output resources the system has open at the same time. This includes actual files open for read/write, but also network sockets that communicate between machines. There is a limit to how many of these descriptors a system can have open at the same time, so a very complicated job or a leaky workload that opens a lot of connections, gets stuck, and does not close can create trouble. Similar to leaky memory, this can lead to performance issues as time goes on.

The Profile tab allows you to see the amount of time spent on executing code, down to the exact function call, on an aggregate level. This can be helpful in identifying tasks that create a bottleneck. Figure 12-11 shows a task duration histogram, which shows a fine-grained view of each task and all the subroutines needed to call for that task, and their runtime. This can help quickly identify a task that is consistently longer than others.

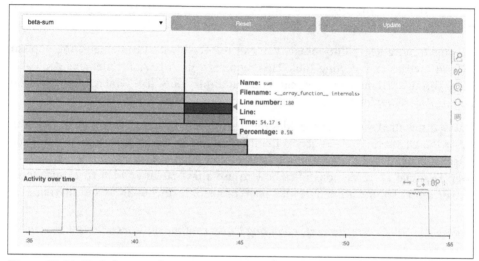

Figure 12-11. Task duration histogram for a Dask job (digital, color version: https://oreil.ly/dIq2o)

 You can change the logging intervals with the `distributed` `.client.scheduler-info-interval` argument within Dask client configurations.

Saving and Sharing Dask Metrics/Performance Logs

You can monitor Dask in real time with the dashboard, but the dashboard will disappear once you close out your cluster. You can save the HTML page, as well as export the metrics as a DataFrame, and write out custom code for metrics (see Example 12-9).

Example 12-9. Generating and saving the Dask dashboard to file

```
from dask.distributed import performance_report

with performance_report(filename="computation_report.html"):
    gnarl = da.random.beta(
        1, 2, size=(
            10000, 10000, 10), chunks=(
            1000, 1000, 5))
    x = da.random.random((10000, 10000, 10), chunks=(1000, 1000, 5))
    y = (da.arccos(x) * gnarl).sum(axis=(1, 2))
    y.compute()
```

You can generate a performance report manually for any block of computation, without having to save the entire runtime report, with the code in Example 12-9. Any computation that you pass within `performance_report("filename")` will be saved under that file. Note that under the hood, this requires Bokeh to be installed.

For much more heavy-duty usage, you can use Dask with Prometheus, the popular Python metrics and alerting tool. This requires you to have Prometheus deployed. Then through Prometheus, you can hook up other tools, like Grafana for visualization or PagerDuty for alerts.

Dask's distributed scheduler provides the metrics info as a task stream object without using the UI itself. You can access the information in the Task Stream UI tab from Dask directly, down to the level of lines of code that you want this to be profiled over. Example 12-10 demonstrates how to use a task stream and then extract some statistics out of it into a small pandas DataFrame for further analysis and sharing.

Example 12-10. Generating and computing Dask's runtime statistics with task stream

```
from dask.distributed import get_task_stream

with get_task_stream() as ts:
    gnarl = da.random.beta(1, 2, size=(100, 100, 10), chunks=(100, 100, 5))
    x = da.random.random((100, 100, 10), chunks=(100, 100, 5))
    y = (da.arccos(x) * gnarl).sum(axis=(1, 2))
    y.compute()
history = ts.data

#display the task stream data as dataframe
history_frame = pd.DataFrame(
    history,
    columns=[
        'worker',
        'status',
        'nbytes',
```

```
          'thread',
          'type',
          'typename',
          'metadata',
          'startstops',
          'key'])

#plot task stream
ts.figure
```

Advanced Diagnostics

You can insert custom metrics using the dask.distributed.diagnostics class. One of the functions here is a MemorySampler context manager. When you run your Dask code within ms.sample(), it records a detailed memory usage on cluster. Example 12-11, while contrived, shows how you would run the same compute over two different cluster configurations and then plot to compare the two different environment configurations.

Example 12-11. Inserting a memory sampler for your code

```
from distributed.diagnostics import MemorySampler
from dask_kubernetes import KubeCluster
from distributed import Client

cluster = KubeCluster()
client = Client(cluster)

ms = MemorySampler()

#some gnarly compute
gnarl = da.random.beta(1, 2, size=(100, 100, 10), chunks=(100, 100, 5))
x = da.random.random((100, 100, 10), chunks=(100, 100, 5))
y = (da.arccos(x) * gnarl).sum(axis=(1, 2))

with ms.sample("memory without adaptive clusters"):
    y.compute()

#enable adaptive scaling
cluster.adapt(minimum=0, maximum=100)

with ms.sample("memory with adaptive clusters"):
    y.compute()

#plot the differences
ms.plot(align=True, grid=True)
```

Scaling and Debugging Best Practices

Here, we discuss some of the commonly identified issues and overlooked considerations when running your code in distributed cluster settings.

Manual Scaling

If your cluster manager supports it, you can scale up and down the number of workers by calling `scale` with the desired number of workers. You can also tell the Dask scheduler to wait until the requested number of workers are allocated and then proceed with computation with the `client.wait_for_workers(n_workers)` command. This can be useful for training certain ML models.

Adaptive/Auto-scaling

We briefly touched on adaptive scaling in previous chapters. You can enable auto/adaptive scaling on your cluster by calling `adapt()` on the Dask client. The scheduler analyzes the computation and invokes the `scale` command to add or remove workers. The Dask cluster types—KubeCluster, PBSCluster, LocalClusters, etc.—are the cluster classes that handle actual requests and scaling up and down of the workers. If you see issues with adaptive scaling, ensure that your Dask is correctly asking for resources from the cluster manager. Of course, for auto-scaling in Dask to work, you have to be able to scale your own resource allocations within the cluster that you are running your job on, be it HPC, managed cloud, etc. We already introduced adaptive scaling in Example 12-11; refer to that example for code snippets.

Persist and Delete Costly Data

Some intermediate results can be used further down in the code execution, but not immediately after. In these cases, Dask might delete the data, not realizing it will need it further down, and you will end up needing another round of costly computation. If you identify this pattern, you can use the `.persist()` command. With this command, you should also use Python's built-in `del` command to ensure that the data is removed when it's no longer needed.

Dask Nanny

Dask Nanny is a process that manages workers. Its job is to prevent workers from exceeding its resource limits, leading to an unrecoverable machine state. It constantly monitors CPU and memory usage for the worker and triggers memory clean-up and compaction. If the worker reaches a bad state, it will automatically restart the worker and try to recover the previous state.

Complications may arise if a worker that contains a computationally expensive and large chunk of data is lost for some reason. The nanny will restart the worker and try to redo the work that led to that point. During that, other workers will also hold on to data that they were working on, leading to a spike in memory usage. The strategies to remedy this will vary, from disabling the nanny to modifying chunking sizes, worker size, and so on. If this happens often, you should consider persisting, or writing that data to disk.[8]

If you see error messages such as "Worker exceeded 95% memory budget. Restarting," nanny is likely where it came from. It's the class responsible for starting workers, monitoring, terminating, and restarting the workers. This memory fraction, as well as spillover location, can be set in the *distributed.yaml* configuration file. HPC users can turn the nanny's memory monitoring off if the system itself has its own memory management strategies. If the system also restarts killed jobs, you could turn off the nanny with the --no-nanny option.

Worker Memory Management

By default, when the worker's memory is around 60% full, it starts sending some data to disk. At over 80%, it stops allocating new data. At 95%, the worker is terminated preemptively, in order to avoid running out of memory. This means after your worker's memory is more than 60% full, there will be performance degradations, and it's usually best practice to keep memory pressure lower.

Advanced users can use Active Memory Manager, a daemon that optimizes memory usage of workers on a holistic view of the cluster. You give this manager a particular goal to optimize for, such as reducing replication of the same data within the cluster, or retire_workers, a special advanced use case where you do memory transfer from one worker to another when the worker is being retired, or other custom policies. In some cases, Active Memory Manager has been shown to decrease memory usage up to 20% for the same task.[9]

---

8 There is a knob you can use to control how fast precedent tasks complete. Sometimes running all the easy tasks too fast might cause you to end up with a lot of intermediate data that is piled up for the later step to go through, leading to undesirable high memory saturation. Look at the documentation related to distributed .scheduler.worker-saturation for more information.

9 You can find out more about it in Dask's documentation (*https://oreil.ly/MhMHf*).

Cluster Sizing

Auto/adaptive scaling takes care of the question of "how many" workers but not of "how big" each worker should be. That said, here are some general rules of thumb:

- Use smaller worker size when debugging, unless you expect that the bug is due to the large number of workers given.

- Size up worker memory allocation with the input data size and number of workers you are using.

- The number of chunks in the data should roughly match the number of workers. Fewer workers than chunks will lead to some chunks not being worked on until the first round of computation is over, leading to a larger memory footprint of intermediate data. Conversely, having more workers than the number of chunks will result in idling workers.

- If you have the option of having higher worker count and smaller individual worker memory (versus smaller worker count and larger individual worker memory), analyze your data's chunk sizes. That chunk must fit in one worker with some room for computation, setting the minimum memory needed for your worker.

Fine-tuning your machine sizes can become a never-ending exercise, so it's important to know what "good enough" is for your purposes.

Chunking, Revisited

We have briefly covered chunks and chunk sizes in earlier chapters. Now we expand on this to cluster scale. Chunk size and worker sizes are integral to how Dask functions, as it uses a block-level view of computation and data within its task graph–based execution model. It's the essential parameter that determines how the distributed computation will work. While using Dask and other distributed systems, we find this is one of the essential ideas to keep in mind as we turn the knobs and dials of such large machines.

For any given worker hardware configuration and computation you are doing, there will be a sweet spot for the chunk sizes, and the user's job is to set this size. Finding the exact number might not be useful, but finding roughly what type of configuration is likely to give you the best result can make a huge difference.

The key idea of chunking is to load balance computation and storage, at a cost of overhead of communications. On one end of the extreme, you have single-machine data engineering, with your data in one pandas DataFrame, or a single Dask Data-Frame with no partitioning. There is not much communication cost, as all communication happens between your RAM and your GPU or CPU, with data moving through a single computer's motherboard. As your data size grows, this monolithic block will not work, and you run into out-of-memory errors, losing all your previous in-memory computation. Hence, you would use a distributed system like Dask.

On the other extreme, a very fragmented dataset with small chunk sizes over multiple machines connected over Ethernet cables will be slower to work together as the communication overhead grows, and may even overrun the scheduler's capacity to handle communications, gathering, and coordinating. Maintaining a happy balance between the two extremes, and knowing which problem requires which tools, is an essential job of modern distributed data engineering.

Avoid Rechunking

When pipelining multiple data streams into a job, you might have two datasets, with two different chunk sizes, even if their data dimensions match. In runtime, Dask will have to rechunk one of the datasets to match the chunk sizes of the other. Doing so in runtime can get costly and memory inefficient. If this is spotted, you can consider having a separate job that does the rechunking before ingesting into your job.

Scheduled Jobs

There are many different systems to make your jobs run on a schedule. This schedule can range from being periodic and time-based to being triggered by upstream events (like data becoming available). Popular tools to schedule jobs include Apache Airflow, Flyte, Argo, GitHub Actions, and Kubeflow.[10] Airflow and Flyte have built-in support for Dask, which can simplify running your scheduled task, so we think that they are both excellent options for scheduled Dask jobs. The built-in operators make it easier to track failure, which is important, as taking actions on stale data can be as bad as taking actions on wrong data.

We also often see people use Unix crontabs and schtasks, but we advise against that, as they run on a single machine and require substantial additional work.

 For scheduled jobs on Kubernetes, you can also have your scheduler create a DaskJob resource (*https://oreil.ly/Uw5Rp*), which will run your Dask program inside the cluster.

In Appendix A, you will learn details about testing and validation, which are especially important for scheduled and automated jobs, where there is no time for manual checking.

---

10 Holden is a co-author of *Kubeflow for Machine Learning* (O'Reilly), so she is biased here.

Deployment Monitoring

Like many other distributed libraries, Dask provides logs, and you can configure Dask logs to be sent to a storage system. The method will vary by the deployment environment and if you are using Jupyter.

One generic way you can get the worker and scheduler logs is through `get_worker_logs()` and `get_scheduler_logs()` on the Dask client. You can specify specific topics and log to/read from just the relevant topics. Refer to Example 9-6 for more information.

You are not limited to logging strings, and you can instead log structured events. This can be especially useful for performance analysis or for anything where the log messages might be visualized rather than looked at individually by a human. In Example 12-12, we do this with a distributed `softmax` function, and log the events and retrieve them on the client.

Example 12-12. Structured logging on workers

```
from dask.distributed import Client, LocalCluster

client = Client(cluster)  # Connect to distributed cluster and override default

d = {'x': [3.0, 1.0, 0.2], 'y': [2.0, 0.5, 0.1], 'z': [1.0, 0.2, 0.4]}
scores_df = dd.from_pandas(pd.DataFrame(data=d), npartitions=1)


def compute_softmax(partition, axis=0):
    """ computes the softmax of the logits
    :param logits: the vector to compute the softmax over
    :param axis: the axis we are summing over
    :return: the softmax of the vector
    """
    if partition.empty:
        return
    import timeit
    x = partition[['x', 'y', 'z']].values.tolist()
    start = timeit.default_timer()
    axis = 0
    e = np.exp(x - np.max(x))
    ret = e / np.sum(e, axis=axis)
    stop = timeit.default_timer()
    partition.log_event("softmax", {"start": start, "x": x, "stop": stop})
    dask.distributed.get_worker().log_event(
        "softmax", {"start": start, "input": x, "stop": stop})
    return ret
```

```
scores_df.apply(compute_softmax, axis=1, meta=object).compute()
client.get_events("softmax")
```

Conclusion

In this chapter, you've learned the various deployment options for Dask distributed, from commodity cloud to HPC infrastructures. You've also learned Jupyter magics to simplify getting access to information with remote deployments. In our experience, Dask on Kubernetes and Dask on Ray on Kubernetes offer the flexibility we need. Your own decision about how to deploy Dask may be different, especially if you are working in a larger institution with existing cluster deployments. Most of the deployment options are covered in detail in the "Deploy Dask Clusters" guide (*https://oreil.ly/j8ueU*), with the notable exception of Dask on Ray, which is covered in the Ray documentation (*https://oreil.ly/hN3Tk*).

You've also learned about runtime considerations and metrics to track when running a distributed work, and the various tools in Dask's dashboard to accomplish that, expanded with more advanced user-defined metrics generation. Using these metrics, you've learned the conceptual basis for tuning your Dask Distributed clusters, troubleshooting, and how this relates to the fundamental design principle of Dask and distributed computing.

Key System Concepts for Dask Users

We've covered a few distributed system concepts briefly as needed in this book, but as you get ready to head out on your own, it's a good idea to review some of the core concepts that Dask is built on. In this appendix, you will learn more about the key principles used in Dask and how they impact the code you write on top of Dask.

Testing

Testing is an often overlooked part of data science and data engineering. Some of our tools, like SQL and Jupyter notebooks, do not encourage testing or make it easy to test—but this does not absolve us of the responsibility to test our code. Data privacy concerns can add another layer of challenge, where we don't want to store user data for testing, requiring us to put in the effort to create "fake" data for testing or break our code down into testable components where we don't need user data.

Manual Testing

We often perform some kind of manual testing while writing software or data tools. This can include simply running the tool and eyeballing the results to see if they look reasonable. Manual testing is time-consuming and not automatically repeatable, so while it is great during development, it is insufficient for long-lived projects.

Unit Testing

Unit testing refers to testing individual units of code rather than the whole system together. This requires having your code be composed in different units, like modules or functions. While this is less common with notebooks, we believe that structuring your code for testability is a good practice to follow.

Writing unit tests for notebooks can be challenging; doctests are slightly easier to inline within a notebook. If you want to use traditional unit test libraries, the ipython-unittest magics (*https://oreil.ly/yUxXy*) let you inline your unit tests within your notebook.

Integration Testing

Integration testing refers to testing how different parts of a system work together. It is often much closer to the real usage of your code, but it can be more complicated, as it involves setting up other systems to test against. You can (to an extent) use some of the same libraries for integration testing, but these tests tend to involve more setup and teardown work.[1] Integration testing is also more likely to be "flaky," since making sure that all of the different components your software needs are present in your test environment before starting the tests can be challenging.

Test-Driven Development

Test-driven development involves taking the requirements or expectations of your code and writing tests and then writing the code after. For data science pipelines this can often be done by creating a sample input (sometimes called a golden set) and writing out what you expect the output to be. Test-driven development can be complicated, especially when integrating multiple data sources.

While you don't need to use test-driven development, we believe it's important to make tests alongside the development of your data pipelines. Tests added after development are better than no tests, but in our experience the context you have during the development helps you create better tests (and validate your assumptions early on).

Property Testing

Property testing is a potentially great solution to the challenge of coming up with test data that covers all of the edge cases in terms of data that your code could trip up on. Instead of writing the traditional "for input A, result B is expected," you specify properties, like "if we have 0 customers, we should have 0 sales" or "all (valid) customers should have a fraud score after this pipeline."

Hypothesis (*https://oreil.ly/zQhnh*) is the most popular library for property testing in Python.

---

1 This can include creating a database, filling it with data, starting up cluster services, etc.

Working with Notebooks

Testing notebooks is painful, which is unfortunate given their immense popularity. Generally, you can either have your testing outside of the notebook, which allows you the use of existing Python testing libraries, or try to put it inside the notebook.

Out-of-Notebook Testing

The traditional option (besides ignoring testing) is to refactor the parts of your code you want to test into separate regular Python files and test those using normal testing libraries. While the partial refactoring can be painful, rewriting to more testable components can bring benefits to debugging as well.

The testbook project (*https://oreil.ly/3_YsK*) is an alternative to refactoring that takes an interesting approach, allowing you to write your tests outside of your notebook, and not requiring you to give up on notebooks. Instead, you use the libraries decorator to annotate tests—for example, `@testbook('untitled_7.ipynb', execute=True)` will import and execute the notebook before executing the test. You can also control which parts of the notebook are executed, but this partial execution can be brittle and prone to breakage on updates.

In-Notebook Testing: In-Line Assertions

Some people like to use in-line assertions in their notebooks as a form of testing. In this case, if something fails (e.g., the assertion that there should be some customers), the rest of the notebook will not run. While we think that having in-line assertions is great, we don't believe it is a replacement for traditional testing.

Data and Output Validation

While good testing can catch many problems, sometimes the real world is more creative than we can ever be, and our code will still fail. In many situations, the worst case is that our program fails and produces an incorrect output that we don't know is incorrect, and then we (or others) take action based on its results. Validation attempts to notify us when our job has failed so that we can take action on it before someone else does. In many ways, it is like running spell-check on a term paper before submission—if there are a few errors, OK, but if everything is red, it's probably good to double-check. Depending on what your job does, validating it will be different.

There are a number of different tools you can use to validate the output of your Dask job, including of course Dask itself. Some tools, like TFX's data validation (*https://oreil.ly/Vfb1Z*), attempt to compare previous versions for statistical similarity and schema changes.[2] Pydantic (*https://oreil.ly/RN8aI*) is relatively new, but it has Dask integration and does excellent type and schema validation. You can also do more complex statistical assertions using its Hypothesis component (which is different from Python's Hypothesis).

ML models can be more difficult to validate without impacting users, but statistical techniques can still help (as can incremental deployments). Since ML models are produced from data, a good (partial) step can be validating the data.

It is useful to think of what the implications could be of your pipeline failing. For example, you might want to spend more time validating a pipeline that determines dosages of medicine in a clinical trial, compared to a job that predicts which version of your ad will be the most successful.[3]

Peer-to-Peer Versus Centralized Distributed

Even inside of a distributed system, there are various levels of "distributed." Dask is a centralized distributed system, where there is a static leader node responsible for various tasks and coordination among the workers. In more distributed systems, there is no static leader node, and if the head node goes away, the remaining peers can elect a new head node, like with ZooKeeper. In even more distributed systems, there is no head node distinction, and all of the nodes in the cluster are effectively equally capable (from a software point of view; the hardware may be different).

Centralized distributed systems tend to be faster, while encountering limitations earlier in terms of scaling and challenges around the failure of the centralized component.

Methods of Parallelism

There are many different ways to split up our work, and in this book we've mostly looked at task and data parallelism.

Task Parallelism

dask.delayed and Python's multi-processing both represent task parallelism. With task parallelism, you are not limited to executing the same code. Task parallelism offers the most flexibility but requires more changes to your code to take advantage of it.

---

2 We do not recommend TFX for new environments, as it can be challenging to get running.

3 We acknowledge that society is often not structured this way.

Data Parallelism

Data parallelism refers to taking the same operation and running it in parallel on different chunks (or partitions) of data. This is a wonderful technique for operations on DataFrames and arrays. Data parallelism depends on partitioning to split up the work. We cover partitioning in detail in Chapter 4.

Shuffles and narrow versus wide transformations

Narrow transformations (or data parallelism without any aggregation or shuffle) are often much faster than *wide* transformations, which involve shuffles or aggregations. While this terminology is borrowed from the Spark community, the distinction (and implications for fault tolerance) applies to Dask's data-parallel operations as well.

Limitations

Data parallelism is not well suited to many different kinds of work. Even when working on data problems, it is not as well suited to doing many different things (non-uniform computation). Data parallelism is often poorly suited to computation on small amounts of data—for example, model serving where you may need to evaluate a single request at a time.

Load Balancing

Load balancing is another way of looking at parallelism where a system (or systems) routes the requests (or tasks) to different servers. Load balancing can range from basic, like round-robin, to "smart," taking advantage of information about the relative load, resources, and data on the workers/servers to schedule the task. The more complex the load balancing is, the more work the load balancer has to do. In Dask all of this load balancing is handled centrally, which requires that the head node has a relatively complete view of most workers' state to intelligently assign tasks.

The other extreme is "simple" load balancing, where some systems, like DNS round-robin-based load balancing (not used in Dask), do not have any information about the system loads and just pick the "next" node. When tasks (or requests) are roughly equal in complexity, round-robin-based load balancing can work well. This technique is most often used for handling web requests or external API requests where you don't have a lot of control over the client making the requests. You are most likely to see this in model serving, like translating text or predicting fraudulent transactions.

Network Fault Tolerance and CAP Theorem

If you search for "distributed computing concepts," you will likely come across the CAP theorem. The CAP theorem is most relevant for distributed data stores, but it's useful to understand regardless. The theorem states that we cannot build a distributed system that is consistent, available, and partition-tolerant. Partitions can occur from hardware failure or, more commonly, from overloaded network links.

Dask itself has already made the trade-off of not being partition-tolerant; whichever side of a network partition has the "leader" is the side that continues on, and the other side is unable to progress.

It's important to understand how this applies to the resources that you are accessing from Dask. For example, you may find yourself in a case in which a network partition means that Dask is unable to write its output. Or—even worse, in our opinion—it can result in situations in which the data you store from Dask is discarded.[4]

The Jepsen project (*https://jepsen.io*), by Kyle Kingsbury, is one of the best projects that we know of for testing distributed storage and query systems.

Recursion (Tail and Otherwise)

Recursion refers to functions that call themselves (either directly or indirectly). When it's indirect, it's called *co-recursion*, and recursive functions that return the final value are called *tail-recursive*.[5] Tail-recursive functions are similar to loops, and sometimes the language can translate tail-recursive calls into loops or maps.

Recursive functions are sometimes avoided in languages that cannot optimize them, since there is overhead to calling a function. Instead, users will try to express the recursive logic using loops.

Excessive non-optimized recursion can result in a stack overflow error. In C, Java, C++, and more, stack memory is allocated separately from the main memory (also called heap memory). In Python, the amount of recursion is controlled by set recursionlimit. Python provides a tail-recursive annotation (*https://oreil.ly/QTHYz*) that you can use to help optimize these recursive calls.

In Dask, while recursive calls don't have the exact same stack problem, excessive recursion can be one of the causes of load on the head node. This is because scheduling the recursive call must pass through the head node, and the excessive number of recursive functions will cause Dask's scheduler to slow down long before any stack size issues are countered.

---

4 This is not the most common fault tolerance of databases, but some default configurations of common databases can result in this.

5 *Indirect* here means with another function in between; for example, "A calls B, which calls A" is an example of co-recursion.

Versioning and Branching: Code and Data

Versioning is an important computer science concept, and it can be applied to both code and data. Ideally, versioning makes it easy to undo errors and go back to earlier versions or explore multiple directions simultaneously. Many of the items we produce are a combination of both our code and our data; to truly meet the goal of being able to quickly roll back and support experimentation, you will want to have versioning for both your code and your data.

Version control tools for source code have existed for a long time. For code, Git (*https://git-scm.com*) has become the most popular open source version control system in usage, overtaking tools such as Subversion, Concurrent Version Systems, and many others.

While understanding Git thoroughly can be very complicated,[6] for common usage there are a few core commands (*https://oreil.ly/ZYBJM*) that often see you through. Teaching Git is beyond the scope of this appendix, but there are a great many resources, including *Head First Git* by Raju Gandhi (O'Reilly) and *Oh Shit, Git!* by Julia Evans, as well as free online resources.

Unfortunately, software version control tools don't currently have the best notebook integration experience and often require additional tools like ReviewNB (*https://www.reviewnb.com*) to make the changes understandable.

Now, a natural question is, can you use the same tools for versioning your data as your software? Sometimes you can—provided that your data is small enough and does not contain any personal information, using source control on data can be OK. However, software tends to be stored in text and is normally relatively smaller than your data, and many of the source control tools do not work well when files start to exceed even a few dozen MBs.

Instead, tools like LakeFS (*https://lakefs.io*) add Git-like versioning semantics on top of existing external data stores (e.g., S3, HDFS, Iceberg, Delta).[7] Another option is to make copies of your tables manually, but we find this leads to the familiar "-final2-really-final" problem with naming notebooks and Word docs.

Isolation and Noisy Neighbors

So far, we've talked about isolation in the context of being able to have your Python packages, but there are more kinds of isolation. Some other levels of isolation include

---

6 One classic XKCD comic (*https://oreil.ly/9zAmg*) comes surprisingly close to capturing our early experiences with Git.

7 Conflict-of-interest disclosure: Holden has received a T-shirt and stickers from the LakeFS project. Some alternatives include Project Nessie (focused on Iceberg tables).

CPU, GPU, memory, and network.[8] Many cluster managers do not provide full isolation—this means that if your tasks get scheduled on the wrong nodes, they might have bad performance. A common solution to this is to request the amounts of resources in-line with the full node to avoid having other jobs scheduled alongside your own.

Strict isolation can also have downsides, especially if the isolation framework doesn't support bursting. Strict isolation without bursting can result in resource waste, but for mission-critical workflows this is often the trade-off.

Machine Fault Tolerance

Fault tolerance is a key concept in distributed computing because the more computers you add, the higher the probability of a fault on any given computer. In some smaller deployments of Dask, machine fault tolerance is not as important, so if you're running Dask exclusively in local mode or on two or three computers you keep under your desk, you might be OK to skip this section.[9]

Dask's core fault tolerance approach is to re-compute lost data. This is the approach chosen by many modern data-parallel systems since failures are not super common, so making the situation with no failures fast is the priority.[10]

It is important to consider, with fault tolerance of Dask, what the fault condition possibilities are in the components Dask is connected to. While re-compute is a fine approach for distributed computing, distributed storage has different trade-offs.

Dask's approach to re-compute on failure means that the data that Dask used for the computation remains present to re-load when needed. In most systems, this will be the case, but in some streaming systems you may need to configure longer TTLs or otherwise have a buffer on top to provide the reliability that Dask requires. Also, if you are deploying your own storage layer (e.g., MinIO), it's important that you deploy it in a way to minimize data loss.

Dask's fault tolerance does not extend to the leader node. A partial solution to this is often called high availability, where a system outside of Dask monitors and restarts your Dask leader node.

Fault tolerance techniques are often also used when scaling down, since fault tolerance and scale down both involve the loss of a node.

---

8 For example, two ML tasks on the same node may both try to use all of the CPU resources.

9 We choose three here since the probability of the failure of a worker node that does not have the driver is only 2x that of the driver (which we can't recover from), and this scales linearly as you add more machines.

10 You can cache intermediate steps to reduce the cost of re-computing, but this only works if the cached location has not failed and requires you to clean up any caching.

Scalability (Up and Down)

Scalability refers to the ability of a distributed system to grow to handle larger problems and the sometimes overlooked ability to shrink when the needs are reduced (say, after the grad students go to sleep). In computer science, we generally categorize scalability as either *horizontal* or *vertical*. Horizontal scaling refers to adding more computers, whereas vertical scaling refers to using bigger computers.

Another important consideration is *auto*-scaling versus *manual* scaling. In auto-scaling, the execution engine (in our case, Dask) will scale the resources for us. Dask's auto-scaler will horizontally scale by adding your workers when needed (provided the deployment supports it). To scale up vertically, you can add larger instance types to Dask's auto-scaler and request those resources with your jobs.

 In a way, Dask's task "stealing" can be viewed as a form of automatic vertical scaling. If a node is incapable of (or especially slow at) handling a task, then another Dask worker can "steal" the task. In practice, the auto-scaler does not allocate higher resource nodes unless you schedule a task that asks for those resources.

Cache, Memory, Disk, and Networking: How the Performance Changes

Dask jobs are frequently data-heavy, and the cost of transferring data to the CPU (or GPU) can have a large impact on performance. CPU cache is normally more than an order of magnitude faster than reading from memory. Reading data from an SSD is roughly 4x slower than memory, and sending data within a data center can be ~10 times slower.[11] CPU caches can normally contain only a few elements.

Transferring data from RAM (or even worse, from disk/network) can result in the CPU stalling or not being able to do any useful work. This makes chaining operations especially important.

The Computers Are Fast website (*https://oreil.ly/Iyzds*) does an excellent job of illustrating these performance impacts with real code.

Hashing

Hashing is an important part not only of Dask but also of computer science in general. Dask uses hashing to convert complex data types into integers to assign the data to the correct partition. Hashing is generally a "one-way" operation that

---

11 Exact performance numbers depend on your hardware.

embeds the larger key space into a smaller key space. For many operations, like assigning data to the correct partitions, you want hashing to be fast. However, for tasks like pseudonymization and passwords, you intentionally choose slower hashing algorithms and frequently add more iterations to make it more difficult to reverse. It's important to pick the right hashing algorithm to match your purposes, since the different behaviors could be a feature in one use case but a bug in the other.

Data Locality

Data transfer costs can quickly overwhelm data compute costs for simple computation. When possible, scheduling tasks on nodes that already have the data is often much faster since the task has to be scheduled somewhere (e.g., you pay the network cost of copying the task regardless), but you can avoid moving the data if you put the task in the right place. Network copies are also generally slower than disk.

Dask allows you to specify a desired worker in your `client.submit` with `workers=`. Also, if you have data that is going to be accessed everywhere, rather than doing a regular scatter, you can broadcast it by adding `broadcast=True` so that all workers have a full copy of the collection.

Exactly Once Versus At Least Once

In most software development the concept of *exactly once* is so much of a given that we don't even think of it as a requirement. For example, doubly applied debits or credits to a bank account could be catastrophic. Exactly-once execution in Dask requires the use of external systems because of Dask's approach to fault tolerance. A common approach is to use a database (distributed or non-distributed) along with transactions to ensure exactly-once execution.

Not all distributed systems have this challenge. Systems in which the inputs and outputs are controlled and fault tolerance is achieved by redundant writes have an easier time with exactly-once execution. Some systems that use re-compute on failure are still able to offer exactly-once execution by integrating distributed locks.

Conclusion

Distributed systems are fun, but as you can see from the distributed systems concepts, they add a substantial amount of overhead. If you don't need distributed systems, then using Dask in local mode and using local data stores can greatly simplify your life. Regardless of whether you decide on local mode or distributed, having an understanding of general systems concepts will help you build better Dask pipelines.

Scalable DataFrames: A Comparison and Some History

Dask's distributed pandas-like DataFrame is, in our opinion, one of its key features. Various approaches exist to provide scalable DataFrame-like functionality. One of the big things that made Dask's DataFrames stand out is the high level of support of the pandas APIs, which other projects are rapidly trying to catch up on. This appendix compares some of the different current and historical DataFrame libraries.

To understand the differences, we will look at a few key factors, some of which are similar to techniques we suggest in Chapter 8. The first one is what the API looks like, and how much of your existing skills and code using pandas can be transferred. Then we'll look at how much work is forced to happen on a single thread, on the driver/head node, and then on a single worker node.

Scalable DataFrames does not have to mean distributed, although distributed scaling often allows for affordable handling of larger datasets than the single-machine options—and at truly massive scales, it's the only practical option.

Tools

One of the common dependencies you'll see in many of the tools is that they are built on top of ASF Arrow. While Arrow is a fantastic project, and we hope to see its continued adoption, it has some type differences (*https://oreil.ly/VPyAL*), especially with respect to nullability.[1] These differences mean that most of the systems built using Arrow share some common restrictions.

Open Multi-Processing (OpenMP) and Open Message Passing Interface (OpenMPI) are two other common dependencies many of these tools depend on. Despite their similar acronyms, by which you'll see them referred to most commonly, they take fundamentally different approaches to parallelism. OpenMP is a single-machine tool focused on shared memory (with potentially non-uniform access). OpenMPI supports multiple machines and instead of shared memory uses message passing (conceptually similar to Dask's actor system) for parallelization.

One Machine Only

The one-machine scalable DataFrames focus on either parallelizing computation or allowing data to not all reside in memory at the same time (e.g., some can reside on disk). To a certain extent, this "data can reside on disk" approach can be solved with swap files at the OS level, but in practice having the library do intelligent paging in and out of elements has its benefits.

Pandas

It may seem silly to mention pandas in a section on scaling DataFrames, but it's useful to remember what the baseline is that we're comparing against. Pandas is, generally, single threaded and requires that all of the data fits in memory on a single machine. There are various tricks that you can use to handle larger datasets in pandas, such as creating huge swap files or serially processing smaller chunks. It's good to note that many of these techniques are incorporated in the tools for scaling pandas, so if you need to do that, it's probably time to start exploring the options to scale. On the other hand, if everything is working fine in pandas, you get 100% pandas API compatibility by using pandas itself, something none of the other options are able to guarantee. Also, pandas is a direct requirement more than any of the scalable pandas tools are (*https://oreil.ly/IzYDb*).

H2O's DataTable

DataTable is a single-machine DataFrame-like attempt to scale processing up to 100 GB (while the project authors describe this as "big data," we view it as more along the lines of medium-sized data). Despite being for Python, DataTable, instead of copying the pandas APIs, aims to inherit much of R's `data.table` APIs. This can make it a great choice for a team coming from R, but for dedicated pandas users it is

---

1 Arrow allows all data types to be null. Pandas does not allow integer columns to contain nulls. When reading Arrow files as pandas, if an Int column does not contain nulls, it will be read as Int in the pandas DataFrame, but if at runtime it encounters a null, the entire column will be read as a float.

likely less appealing. DataTable is also a single-company open source project, residing under H2O's GitHub rather than in a foundation or on its own. At the time of this writing, it has a relatively concentrated location of developer activity (*https://oreil.ly/ 8vgA5*). It has active CI (being run on incoming PRs), which we believe suggests higher-quality software. DataTable can use OpenMP to parallelize computation on a single machine, but it does not require OpenMP.

Polars

Polars is another single-machine scalable DataFrame, but it takes the approach of writing its core functionality in Rust instead of C/C++ or Fortran. Like many of the distributed DataFrame tools, polars uses the ASF's Arrow project for storing the DataFrames. Similarly, polars uses lazy evaluation to pipeline operations and internally partition/chunk the DataFrame, so (most of the time) it needs to have only a subset of the data in memory at any one time. Polars has one of the largest developer communities among all single-machine scalable DataFrames (*https://oreil.ly/zxoFJ*). Polars links to benchmarks from its main page, showing it to be substantially faster than many of the distributed tools—but this comparison makes sense only when the distributed tools are constrained to a single machine, which is unlikely. It achieves its parallelism by using all of the cores in a single machine. Polars has extensive documentation (*https://oreil.ly/QW5s2*), and it also has an explicit section on what to expect when coming from regular pandas. Not only does it have CI, but it has also integrated benchmark testing as part of each PR and tests against multiple versions of Python and environments.

Distributed

The majority of tools for scaling DataFrames are distributed in nature, since all of the fancy tricks on a single machine can get you only so far.

ASF Spark DataFrame

Spark started out with what it called a resilient distributed dataset (RDD) and then quickly added a more DataFrame-like API called DataFrames. This caused much excitement, but many folks interpreted it to mean "pandas-like," whereas Spark's (initial) DataFrames was more akin to "SQL-like" DataFrames. Spark is written primarily in Scala and Java, both of which run on the Java Virtual Machine (JVM). While Spark has a Python API, it involves substantial data transfer between the JVM and Python, which can be slow and can increase memory requirements. Spark DataFrames was created before ASF Arrow, and so it has its own in-memory storage format, but it has since added support for using Arrow for communication between the JVM and Python.

PySpark errors are especially difficult to debug, since when anything goes wrong you get a Java exception along with a Python exception.

SparklingPandas

Since Holden co-wrote SparklingPandas, it is the one library we can confidently say not to use without having to worry about people being upset.[2] SparklingPandas is built on top of ASF Spark's RDD and DataFrame APIs to provide a more Python-like API, but as the logo is a panda eating bamboo on a sticky note, you can see that we didn't get all the way. SparklingPandas did show it was possible to provide a pandas-like experience by reusing parts of pandas itself.

For embarrassingly parallel types of operations, adding each function from the pandas API by using map to delegate the Python code on each DataFrame was very fast. Some operations, like dtypes, were evaluated on just the first DataFrame. Grouped and window operations were more complicated.

Since the initial co-authors had day jobs with other focus areas, the project failed to move beyond proof-of-concept.

Spark Koalas/Spark pandas DataFrames

The Koalas project, which was integrated into Spark 3.2, initially came out of Databricks. Koalas follows a similar approach of chunking pandas DataFrames, but these DataFrames are represented as Spark DataFrames rather than Arrow DataFrames. Like most of the systems, the DataFrames are lazily evaluated to allow for pipelining. Arrow is used to transfer data to and from the JVM, so you still have all of the type restrictions of Arrow. This project benefits from being part of a large community and being interoperable with much of the traditional big data stack. This comes from being a part of the JVM and Hadoop ecosystem, which also comes with some downsides for performance. At present, moving data between the JVM and Python increases overhead, and in general, Spark is focused on supporting heavier-weight tasks.

Grouped operations on Spark Koalas/Spark pandas DataFrames do not yet support partial aggregations. This means that all the data for one key must fit on one node.

Cylon

Cylon's home page is very focused on benchmarks, but the benchmark it has chosen (comparing Cylon to Spark on a single machine) is one that is easy to meet, since Spark is designed for distributed usage instead of single-machine usage. Cylon uses

---

2 Besides ourselves, and if you're reading this you've likely helped Holden buy a cup of coffee and that's enough. :)

PyArrow for storage along with OpenMPI for managing its task parallelism. Cylon also has a GPU backend called GCylon. PyClon's documentation has a lot of room for growth, and the link to its API documentation is currently broken.

The Cylon community seems to have ~30 messages per year, and attempting to find any open source users of the DataFrame library comes up empty (*https://oreil.ly/uroxr*). The contributor file (*https://oreil.ly/dWC16*) and LinkedIn show the majority of contributors all share a common university.

The project follows several software engineering best practices, like having CI enabled. That being said, the comparatively small (visibly active) community and lack of clear documentation mean that, in our mind, depending on Cylon would be more involved than some other options.

Ibis

The Ibis project promises (*https://oreil.ly/9OL2f*) "the flexibility of Python analytics with the scale and performance of modern SQL." It compiles your somewhat pandas-like code (as much as possible) into SQL. This is convenient, as not only do many big data systems (like Hive, Spark, BigQuery, etc.) support SQL, but it is also the de facto query language for the majority of databases out there. Unfortunately, SQL is not uniformly implemented, so moving between backend engines may result in breakages, but Ibis does a great job of tracking which APIs work with which backends (*https://oreil.ly/g2E_W*). Of course, this design limits you to the kinds of expressions that can be expressed in SQL.

Modin

Like Ibis, Modin is slightly different from many of the other tools in that it has multiple distributed backends, including Ray, Dask, and OpenMPI. Modin has the stated goal of handling from 1 MB to 1+ TB, which is a wide range to attempt to cover. Modin's home page (*https://modin.org*) also makes a claim to "Scale your pandas workflows by changing a single line of code," which, while catchy, in our opinion overpromises on the API compatibility and knowledge required to take advantage of parallel and distributed systems.[3] In our opinion, Modin is very exciting since it seems silly for each distributed computing engine to have its own re-implementation of the pandas APIs. Modin has a very active developer community, with core developers from multiple companies and backgrounds. On the other hand, we feel that the current documentation does not do a good enough job of setting users up for success with understanding the limitations of Modin. Thankfully, much of the intuition you

---

3 For example, see the confusion around the limitation with groupBy + apply, which is not otherwise documented besides a GitHub issue (*https://oreil.ly/rIeam*).

will have developed around Dask DataFrames still applies to Modin. We think Modin is ideal for individuals who need to move between different computation engines.

 Unlike the other systems, Modin is eagerly evaluated, meaning it can't take advantage of automatic pipelining of your computation.

Vanilla Dask DataFrame

We are biased here, but we think that Dask's DataFrame library does an excellent job of striking a balance between being an easy on-ramp and being clear about its limitations. Dask's DataFrames have a large number of contributors from a variety of different companies. Dask DataFrames also have a relatively high level of parallelism, including for grouped operations, not found in many of the other systems.

cuDF

cuDF extends Dask DataFrame to add support for GPUs. It is, however, primarily a single-company project, from NVIDIA. This makes sense since NVIDIA wants to sell you more GPUs, but it also does mean it is unlikely to, say, add support for AMD GPUs anytime soon. This project is likely to be maintained if NVIDIA continues to see a future in selling more GPUs for data analytics as best served with pandas-like interfaces.

cuDF not only has CI but also has a strong culture of code review with per-area responsibilities.

Conclusion

In an ideal world, there would be a clear winner, but as you can see, the different scalable DataFrame libraries serve different purposes, and except those already abandoned, all have potential uses. We think all of these libraries have their place, depending on your exact needs.

Debugging Dask

Depending on your debugging techniques, moving to distributed systems could require a new set of techniques. While you can use debuggers in remote mode, it often requires more setup work. You can also run Dask locally to use your existing debugging tools in many other situations, although—take it from us—a surprising number of difficult-to-debug errors don't show up in local mode. Dask has a special hybrid approach. Some errors happen outside Python, making them more difficult to debug, like container out-of-memory (OOM) errors, segmentation faults, and other native errors.

Some of this advice is common across distributed systems, including Ray and Apache Spark. As such, some elements of this chapter are shared with *High Performance Spark*, second edition, and *Scaling Python with Ray*.

Using Debuggers

There are a few different options for using debuggers in Dask. PyCharm and PDB both support connecting to remote debugger processes, but figuring out where your task is running and also setting up the remote debugger can be a challenge. For details on PyCharm remote debugging, see the JetBrains article "Remote Debugging with PyCharm" (*https://oreil.ly/HGl90*). One option is to use epdb and run import epdb; epdb.serve() inside of an actor. The easiest option, which is not perfect, is to have Dask re-run failed tasks locally by running client.recreate_error_locally on the future that failed.

General Debugging Tips with Dask

You likely have your own standard debugging techniques for working with Python code, and these are not meant to replace them. Some general techniques that are helpful with Dask include the following:

- Break up failing functions into smaller functions; smaller functions make it easier to isolate the problem.
- Be careful about referencing variables from outside of a function, which can result in unintended scope capture, serializing more data and objects than intended.
- Sample data and try to reproduce locally (local debugging is often easier).
- Use mypy (*https://mypy-lang.org*) for type checking. While we haven't included types in many of our examples for space, in production code liberal type usage can catch tricky errors.
- Having difficulty tracking down where a task is getting scheduled? Dask actors can't move, so use an actor to keep all invocations on one machine for debugging.
- When the issues do appear, regardless of parallelization, debugging your code in local single-threaded mode can make it easier to understand what's going on.

With these tips you will (often) be able to find yourself in a familiar enough environment to use your traditional debugging tools, but some types of errors are a little bit more complicated.

Native Errors

Native errors and core dumps can be challenging to debug for the same reasons as container errors. Since these types of errors often result in the container exiting, accessing the debugging information can become challenging. Depending on your deployment, there may be a centralized log aggregator that collects all of the logs from the containers, although sometimes these can miss the final few parts of the log (which you likely care about the most). A quick solution to this is to add a sleep to the launch script (on failure) so that you can connect to the container (e.g., [dasklaunchcommand] || sleep 100000) and use native debugging tools.

However, accessing the internals of a container can be easier said than done. In many production environments, you may not be able to get remote access (e.g., kubectl exec on Kubernetes) for security reasons. If that is the case, you can (sometimes) add a shutdown script to your container specification that copies the core files to a location that persists after the container shuts down (e.g., s3 or HDFS or NFS). Your cluster administrator may also have recommended tools to help debug (or if not, they may be able to help you create a recommended path for your organization).

Some Notes on Official Advice for Handling Bad Records

Dask's official debugging guide (*https://oreil.ly/I9wDw*) recommends removing failed futures manually. When loading data that can be processed in smaller chunks rather than entire partitions at a time, returning tuples with successful and failed data is better, since removing entire partitions is not conducive to determining the root cause. This technique is demonstrated in Example C-1.

Example C-1. Alternative approach for handling bad data

```
# Handling some potentially bad data; this assumes line-by-line
raw_chunks = bag.read_text(
    urls,
    files_per_partition=1,
    linedelimiter="helloworld")


def maybe_load_data(data):
    try:
        # Put your processing code here
        return (pandas.read_csv(StringIO(data)), None)
    except Exception as e:
        return (None, (e, data))


data = raw_chunks.map(maybe_load_data)
data.persist()
bad_data = data.filter(lambda x: x[0] is None)
good_data = data.filter(lambda x: x[1] is None)
```

> Bad records here does not exclusively mean records that fail to load or parse; they can also be records that are causing your code to fail. By following this pattern, you can extract the problematic records for deeper investigation and use this to improve your code.

Dask Diagnostics

Dask has built-in diagnostic tools for both distributed (*https://oreil.ly/Uin87*) and local (*https://oreil.ly/JO4qR*) schedulers. The local diagnostics are more featureful with pretty much every part of debugging. These diagnostics can be especially great for debugging situations in which you see a slow degradation of performance over time.

It's really easy to accidentally use Dask's distributed local backend by mistake when making a Dask client, so if you don't see the diagnostics you expect, make sure you are explicit about which backend you are running on.

Conclusion

You will have a bit more work to get started with your debugging tools in Dask, and when possible, Dask's local mode offers a great alternative to remote debugging. Not all errors are created equal, and some errors, like segmentation faults in native code, are especially challenging to debug. Good luck finding the bug(s); we believe in you.

Streaming with Streamz and Dask

This book has been focused on using Dask to build batch applications, where data is collected from or provided by the user and then used for calculations. Another important group of use cases are the situations requiring you to process data as it becomes available.[1] Processing data as it becomes available is called streaming.

Streaming data pipelines and analytics are becoming more popular as people have higher expectations from their data-powered products. Think about how you would feel if a bank transaction took weeks to settle; it would seem archaically slow. Or if you block someone on social media, you expect that block to take effect immediately. While Dask excels at interactive analytics, we believe it does not (currently) excel at interactive responses to user queries.[2]

Streaming jobs are different from batch jobs in a number of important ways. They tend to have faster processing time requirements, and the jobs themselves often have no defined endpoint (besides when the company or service is shut down). One situation in which small batch jobs may not cut it includes dynamic advertising (tens to hundreds of milliseconds). Many other data problems may straddle the line, such as recommendations, where you want to update them based on user interactions but a delay of a few minutes is probably (mostly) OK.

As discussed in Chapter 8, Dask's streaming component appears to be less frequently used than other components. Streaming in Dask is, to an extent, added on after the fact,[3] and there are certain places and times when you may notice this. This is most

---

1 Albeit generally with some (hopefully small) delay.

2 While these are both "interactive," the expectations of someone going to your website and placing an order versus those of a data scientist trying to come up with a new advertising campaign are very different.

3 The same is true for Spark streaming, but Dask's streaming is even less integrated than Spark's streaming.

apparent when loading and writing data—everything must move through the main client program and is then either scattered or collected.

 Streamz is not currently capable of handling more data per batch than can fit on the client computer in memory.

In this appendix, you will learn the basics of how Dask streaming is designed, its limitations, and how it compares to some other streaming systems.

 As of this writing, Streamz does not implement `ipython_display` in many places, which may result in error-like messages in Jupyter. You can ignore these (it falls back to `repr`).

Getting Started with Streamz on Dask

Streamz is straightforward to install. It's available from PyPI, and you can use `pip` to install it, although as with all libraries, you must make it available on all the workers. Once you have installed Streamz, you just need to create a Dask client (even in local mode) and import it, as shown in Example D-1.

Example D-1. Getting started with Streamz

```
import dask
import dask.dataframe as dd
from streamz import Stream
from dask.distributed import Client

client = Client()
```

 When there are multiple clients, Streamz uses the most recent Dask client created.

Streaming Data Sources and Sinks

So far in this book, we've loaded data from either local collections or distributed filesystems. While these can certainly serve as sources for streaming data (with some limitations), there are some additional data sources that exist in the streaming world.

Streaming data sources are distinct, as they do not have a defined end, and therefore behave a bit more like a generator than a list. Streaming sinks are conceptually similar to consumers of generators.

 Streamz has limited sink (or write destination) support, meaning in many cases it is up to you to write your data back out in a streaming fashion with your own function.

Some streaming data sources have the ability to replay or look back at messages that have been published (up to a configurable time period), which is especially useful for a re-compute–based approach to fault tolerance. Two of the popular distributed data sources (and sinks) are Apache Kafka and Apache Pulsar, both of which have the ability to look back at previous messages. An example streaming system that lacks this ability is RabbitMQ.

Streamz's API documentation (*https://oreil.ly/LOpPJ*) covers which sources are supported; for simplicity, we will focus here on Apache Kafka and the local iterable source. Streamz does all loading in the head process, and then you must scatter the result. Loading streaming data should look familiar, with loading a local collection shown in Example D-2 and loading from Kafka shown in Example D-3.

Example D-2. Loading a local iterator

```
local_stream = Stream.from_iterable(
    ["Fight",
     "Flight",
     "Freeze",
     "Fawn"])
dask_stream = local_stream.scatter()
```

Example D-3. Loading from Kafka

```
batched_kafka_stream = Stream.from_kafka_batched(
    topic="quickstart-events",
    dask=True, # Streamz will call scatter internally for us
    max_batch_size=2, # We want this to run quickly, so small batches
    consumer_params={
        'bootstrap.servers': 'localhost:9092',
        'auto.offset.reset': 'earliest', # Start from the start
        # Consumer group id
        # Kafka will only deliver messages once per consumer group
        'group.id': 'my_special_streaming_app12'},
    # Note some sources take a string and some take a float :/
    poll_interval=0.01)
```

In both of these examples, Streamz will start reading from the most recent message. If you want Streamz to go back to the start of the messages stored, you would add `` ``.

 Streamz's reading exclusively on a single-head process is a place you may encounter bottlenecks as you scale.

As with the rest of this book, we assume that you are using existing data sources. If that's not the case, we encourage you to check out the Apache Kafka or Apache Pulsar documentation (along with the Kafka adapter), as well as the cloud offerings from Confluent.

Word Count

No streaming section would be complete without word count, but it's important to note that our streaming word count in Example D-4—in addition to the restriction with data loading—could not perform the aggregation in a distributed fashion.

Example D-4. Streaming word count

```
local_wc_stream = (batched_kafka_stream
                   # .map gives us a per batch view, starmap per elem
                   .map(lambda batch: map(lambda b: b.decode("utf-8"), batch))
                   .map(lambda batch: map(lambda e: e.split(" "), batch))
                   .map(list)
                   .gather()
                   .flatten().flatten() # We need to flatten twice.
                   .frequencies()
                   ) # Ideally, we'd call flatten frequencies before the gather,
                     # but they don't work on DaskStream
local_wc_stream.sink(lambda x: print(f"WC {x}"))
# Start processing the stream now that we've defined our sinks
batched_kafka_stream.start()
```

In the preceding example, you can see some of the current limitations of Streamz, as well as some familiar concepts (like map). If you're interested in learning more, refer to the Streamz API documentation (*https://oreil.ly/VpkEz*); note, however, that in our experience, some components will randomly not work on non-local streams.

GPU Pipelines on Dask Streaming

If you are working with GPUs, the cuStreamz project (*https://oreil.ly/QCk7O*) simplifies the integration of cuDF with Streamz. cuStreamz uses a number of custom components for performance, like loading data from Kafka into the GPU instead of having to first land in a Dask DataFrame and then convert it. cuStreamz also implements a custom version of checkpointing with more flexibility than the default Streamz project. The developers behind the project, who are largely employed by people hoping to sell you more GPUs, claim up to an 11x speed-up (*https://oreil.ly/6wUpB*).

Limitations, Challenges, and Workarounds

Most streaming systems have some form of state checkpointing, allowing streaming applications to be restarted from the last checkpoint when the main control program fails. Streamz's checkpointing technique is limited to not losing any unprocessed records, but accumulated state can be lost. It is up to you to build your own state checkpointing/restoration if you are building up state over time. This is especially important as the probability of encountering a single point of failure over a long enough window is ~100%, and streaming applications are often intended to run indefinitely.

This indefinite runtime leads to a number of other challenges. Small memory leaks can add up over time, but you can mitigate them by having the worker restart periodically.

Streaming programs that perform aggregations often have problems with late-arriving data. This means that, while you can define your window however you want, you may have records that *should* have been in that window but did not arrive in time for the process. Streamz has no built-in solution for late-arriving data. Your choices are to manually track the state inside of your process (and persist it somewhere), ignore late-arriving data, or use another stream-processing system with support for late-arriving data (including kSQL, Spark, or Flink).

In some streaming applications it is important that messages are processed exactly once (e.g., a bank account). Dask is generally not well suited to such situations due to re-computing on failure. This similarly applies to Streamz on Dask, where the only option is *at-least-once* execution. You can work around this by using an external system, such as a database, to keep track of which messages have been processed.

Conclusion

In our opinion, Streamz with Dask is off to an interesting start in support of streaming data inside of Dask. Its current limitations make it best suited to situations in which there is a small amount of streaming data coming in. That being said, in many situations the amount of streaming data is much smaller than the amount of batch-oriented data, and being able to stay within one system for both allows you to avoid duplicated code or logic. If Streamz does not meet your needs, there are many other Python streaming systems available. Some Python streaming systems you may want to check out include Ray streaming, Faust, or PySpark. In our experience, Apache Beam's Python API has even more room to grow than Streamz.

Index

About the Authors

Holden Karau is a queer transgender Canadian, Apache Spark committer, Apache Software Foundation member, and active open source contributor. As a software engineer, she's worked on a variety of distributed computing, search, and classification problems at Apple, Google, IBM, Alpine, Databricks, Foursquare, and Amazon. She graduated from the University of Waterloo with a bachelor of mathematics in computer science. Outside of software, she enjoys playing with fire, welding, riding scooters, eating poutine, and dancing.

Mika Kimmins is a data engineer, distributed systems researcher, and ML consultant. She has worked on a variety of NLP, language modeling, reinforcement learning, and ML pipelining at scale as a Siri data engineer at Apple, as an academic, and in not-for-profit engineering capacities. She holds an MS in engineering science and an MBA from Harvard, and a BS in computer science and mathematics from the University of Toronto. As a Korean-Canadian-American trans woman, Mika is active in data-driven advocacy for queer health care access, advises undergraduate computer science students, and attempts to keep her volunteer EMT courses current. Her hobbies include figure skating, aerial arts, and sewing.

Colophon

The animal on the cover of *Scaling Python with Dask* is the spectacled caiman (*Caiman crocodilus*), also known as the white or common caiman.

Despite its species name (*crocodilus*), this small to medium-sized crocodilian is more closely related to the phenotypically similar alligator (being of the family *Alligatoridae*) than the crocodile (family *Crocodylidae*), and is often misidentified as the former. Its common name derives from a protruding, bony ridge between its eyes, which is reminiscent of the bridge between a pair of eyeglasses.

The spectacled caiman is the most widely distributed caiman globally, and the most widely distributed New World crocodilian, with a native range extending throughout much of Central and South America. Populations have also been introduced in the United States, Puerto Rico, and Cuba. Though intolerant of cold climates, the caiman is otherwise quite adaptable and lives in a variety of habitats, including forests and inland wetlands and rivers.

Climate and temperature play an especially important role in caimans' nesting habits. Eggs are typically laid only in the summer months, and the caimans use vegetation to incubate their nests: as the vegetation decays, it produces heat, which keeps the eggs warm. Nest temperature ultimately determines the sex of the developing caimans (around 90°F or higher produces female offspring).

In the 1980s, the spectacled caiman was listed as threatened by the IUCN, due to population declines caused primarily by commercial hunting. Conservation programs for the species are now in place in many countries, and with a large global population and range, the species is now listed as of least concern. Many of the animals on O'Reilly covers are endangered; all of them are important to the world.

The cover illustration is by Karen Montgomery, based on an antique line engraving by Georges Cuvier. The cover fonts are Gilroy Semibold and Guardian Sans. The text font is Adobe Minion Pro; the heading font is Adobe Myriad Condensed; and the code font is Dalton Maag's Ubuntu Mono.

O'REILLY®

Learn from experts.
Become one yourself.

Books | Live online courses
Instant answers | Virtual events
Videos | Interactive learning

Get started at oreilly.com.